CONTENTS

D0674704

GENERAL LEARNING OBJECTIVES OF THIS UNIT

This Open Learning Unit explains the principles of statistical inference and describes how to carry out and interpret various tests of significance for one and for two groups of scores and for tables of frequencies. It contains statistical tables for all the tests that are described. It explains the types of situation where each test is appropriate and describes its advantages and limitations. It equips you to use the tests to analyse your own data and to answer examination questions on them.

By the end of this Unit, you should understand:

> the nature of statistical inference from data;

> the difference between scores and frequencies;

> the difference between one-sample and two-sample tests;

> how to carry out and interpret various tests of significance;

> the advantages and disadvantages of each type of test.

In order to understand this Unit fully, it is necessary to have covered the material in Unit 1, *Models and Methods for the Behavioural Sciences*, and Unit 2, *Describing and Interpreting Data*. Technical terms that are introduced for the first time in this Unit are printed in bold letters and appear in a Glossary at the end. Terms that were introduced in the earlier Units are generally used without further explanation.

Making inferences about populations

KEY AIMS: By the end of Part 1 you should understand:
- ▷ *why statistical inference involves probability;*
- ▷ *the difference between Type 1 and Type 2 errors;*
- ▷ *the nature of Null Hypotheses and Alternative Hypotheses;*
- ▷ *the difference between directional and non-directional tests of significance;*
- ▷ *what significant and non-significant results tell us.*

Albert: The car doesn't sound right. I'll ask the garage to look at it.
Victoria: They'll charge a lot. Can't it wait?
Albert: It's worth it – I don't want it to break down while I'm so busy.

In Unit 1, *Models and Methods for the Behavioural Sciences*, we looked at ways of collecting data to improve our understanding of what living creatures (including ourselves) do and feel. In Unit 2, *Describing and Interpreting Data*, we looked at different ways to describe, organize and summarize that data. And that is the best way to begin the interpretation of any data.

➤ **Describe what you have found before drawing inferences from it.**

Almost always, though, we want to go further than this. Our aim in an investigation is not simply to find out about the particular individuals we studied. They are merely a **sample** from a much larger group and it is the larger group that we really want to know about: all professional musicians in the country, all bus passengers in this area, even, occasionally, all human beings, rather than only those included in any particular study. A wider group to which we hope to generalize our results is called a **population.** (The term is used in statistics to refer to a wider group than the one we measured, but in fact it rarely refers to everyone in the land.) But can we really use information obtained from a small group to tell us about a larger group we did not study?

Sample pool

© Copyright. No photocopying allowed

1

We are justified in generalizing our results and making statements about a target population only if we can draw **statistical inferences** from the sample data. For instance, we might measure the verbal abilities of a group of boys and a group of girls. We could then *describe* the difference between our two groups of scores in various ways, and could do it quite precisely, but that in itself would not tell us about the difference in verbal ability of boys and girls in general. To compare 'boys' and 'girls', rather than this small group of boys and that small group of girls, we need to treat the data we actually obtained as samples and use the data to make a statistical *inference* about the populations of boys and girls in general.

If we test every individual repeatedly, they will not obtain exactly the same scores every time. This means that *even if we are able to test everyone in some particular population* our results are never more than a sample of the measurements we might have made. Thus, in analysing behavioural data, we almost always need statistical inferences so that our conclusions can go beyond the particular scores we happened to collect.

Generalizing from a sample to a population

The trouble with drawing conclusions about populations from data consisting of no more than a sample of the possible measurements is that *we can never be certain that our conclusions are correct.* It's always possible that somewhere among the large number of measurements we didn't make, there are some that mean our conclusions are wrong.

In Unit 2, *Describing and Interpreting Data*, we examined data from a small survey in which Albert and Victoria asked passengers how long they expected to have to wait for a bus and then timed how long the bus took to arrive. In this Unit we will look at some of their data again in order to make statistical inferences about the general population of bus passengers. These generalized conclusions are more interesting and more useful. But our conclusions about the sample were all quite definite: we were able to say categorically that scores of such-and-such a kind were obtained. When we come to make generalizations to the wider population we have to settle for probabilistic statements. We cannot say that such-and-such is so, we can only say things like 'there is only one chance in twenty of getting results like these if there really is no difference in the population'.

Probability and chance

Any conclusion we draw about a population involves **probability.** That is, we can never say categorically that something is true or false but only that there is *some probability* of it being true. This probability can be described mathematically by a number between 0 and 1: 0 indicates that there is no possibility of it being true (the probability is nil) while a probability of 1 indicates that it is certainly true. If we toss a coin, the probability that it falls heads is 0.5 (1 in 2) because there are two possible outcomes that are equally likely. This means that, on average, out of every two tosses, one will be a head.

It is only very rarely that you get ten heads and no tails in ten tosses. The probability of this happening is much smaller; in fact it's about 0.001 (1 in 1000) so it will happen, on average, about once in every thousand times you toss ten coins. But please note that it *can* happen, purely by chance, without any other cause. It is useful to remember this caution when drawing conclusions from any set of data.

Statistical tests

Methods for calculating the probabilities we use when going from samples to populations are called **statistical tests** (also called tests of statistical significance',' significance tests' or 'hypothesis tests') and several are described in this Unit. But before we can use them properly, we need to understand the logic they follow.

➤ **Statistical tests are devices for calculating the probability of getting a particular type of result by chance.**

That is, they test how likely (how probable) it is that results looking as interesting as ours could actually arise just from random (and completely uninteresting) variability in the measurements. If the probability is small, the explanation that chance alone is responsible seems less reasonable. For instance, if we toss a coin ten times and get ten heads and no tails, we probably suspect that something other than chance is involved.

If we want to show that chance is not a good explanation for our results, a *small probability* is what we want. If it is small enough, the result is said to be **statistically significant**. But how do we know when it's small enough?

Type 1 and Type 2 errors

The choice of what size of probability should be considered significant entails a compromise. If we make the target too easy to meet, say 0.1 (1 in 10) we will too often conclude that something is **significant** when only chance is at work. That is called a **Type 1 error**. On the other hand, if we demand a probability that is *too* small, say 0.001 (1 in 1000), we are setting a target that is difficult to reach so we will often fail to conclude that the result is significant even when there is some important effect at work. That is called a **Type 2 error**.

Ideally, we would like to avoid both Type 1 and Type 2 errors, but unfortunately that isn't possible. If we make Type 1 errors less frequent by demanding a very small probability, like 0.001, we increase the number of Type 2 errors. We can reduce the occurrence of Type 2 errors by accepting as significant a larger probability, such as 0.1, but that increases the number of Type 1 errors. Decreasing one error by changing the size of probability considered 'significant' always makes the other error more likely. It seems that we just can't win.

'We've got that funny sound again. Perhaps we should have taken it to the garage.'

The Null Hypothesis

A **Null Hypothesis** is just a precise way of stating that chance alone can account for the results we obtained – any time we use a significance test we are really examining the plausibility of some Null Hypothesis. The Null Hypothesis is used merely for the purpose of argument. There would be little point to an investigation if, at the beginning, we actually believed the Null Hypothesis was true. In fact we usually hope that it is not true and that the **Alternative Hypothesis** (often called the **Experimental Hypothesis**) is correct. The Alternative Hypothesis is the opposite of the Null Hypothesis. The Null Hypothesis says that chance alone is responsible for the results; the Alternative Hypothesis says that 'something' other than chance *has played a part*.

The Alternative Hypothesis does not claim that chance has played no part; nor does it say exactly what is that other 'something' that has affected the results. To be able to decide what, apart from chance, has influenced the outcome requires us to have done the right things when the investigation was being designed and carried out. It is the task of experimental design to ensure that just one satisfactory explanation is left after chance is eliminated.

Interpreting a non-significant result. The probability given by a test of significance is the probability of *obtaining such results if the Null Hypothesis is true*. It does *not* give us the probability of the Null Hypothesis actually being true – and it is particularly important to remember this when interpreting non-significant results. Even if we find that such results can be obtained by chance quite easily, we still can't conclude that chance is likely to be the only cause. Such a test would show that chance *can* easily explain the results but doesn't estimate the probability that it *did* give us the results. A simple example may help.

Suppose you find a coin lying head-up on a table. Did it just fall at random or did someone place it that way up? We know that a coin tossed at random has a probability of 0.5 of landing head-up, so we certainly can't reject the Null Hypothesis that it fell head-up by pure chance – the result is very far from being significant at the 0.05 level. However, the fact that it could easily have fallen head-up by chance does not make you certain that it did so. It could just as easily have been put there carefully by someone.

Contrast that with finding a coin lying *on its edge* on a table. The probability of a coin remaining on edge after falling is tiny, so we feel inclined to reject the Null Hypothesis of a chance result and conclude that someone must have balanced it there. This significant result (a small probability if chance is the only cause) leads us to a definite conclusion: someone put it there. The previous, non-significant result (a high probability, even if chance is the only cause) left us completely uncertain whether someone put it there or it fell randomly.

A significance test lets us conclude *nothing useful at all* if the result is not significant. It is a definite error to conclude that because a result is not significant we have demonstrated the absence of any effect other than chance. Please remember:

> **A significance test cannot tell us that chance is the only explanation for our results**.

SAQ
2

Write a brief explanation of why a Type 1 error is a mistaken conclusion but a Type 2 error is not.

Statistical tests answer a question about the data

Every statistical test answers a question about the data. Although they ask somewhat different questions, each of them contains the following idea: could such results reasonably be obtained by chance? What do we mean by 'such results'? None of the tests described in this Unit considers the probability of only the particular results that were obtained in our study. The probability we use is the total probability of the outcome we observed, *plus all outcomes that would have differed even more from the predictions of the Null Hypothesis.* As we shall see later, all tests take account of:

> the size of the difference;
> the variability of the difference;
> the amount of data.

But each statistical test approaches the task in a different way and each asks a slightly different question if we look deeply enough into it.

Directional (one-tailed) and non-directional (two-tailed) tests

If we are comparing two groups of scores, drawn respectively from populations A and B, three different Null Hypotheses are possible and each has its own Alternative Hypothesis.

NH1: There is no difference between populations A and B. The Alternative Hypothesis is that there is some difference (in either direction).

NH2: Population A is the same as population B or higher. The Alternative Hypothesis is that population B is higher than population A.

NH3: Population A is the same as population B or lower. The Alternative Hypothesis is that population A is higher than population B.

The thing to note here is that Alterative Hypotheses 2 and 3 predict the direction of the difference while Alternative Hypothesis 1 predicts a difference but not its direction.

Mel Calman, from *Calman Revisited*, published by Methuen. Reproduced with permission.

If we test the first Null Hypothesis we have a **non-directional** test, also called a **two-sided** or **two-tailed** test. If we test Null Hypothesis 2 or 3 we have a **directional** test, also called a **one-sided** or **one-tailed** test because we are testing for a difference in a specified direction.

A difference of a given size in our data will give a more significant result in a directional test than in a non-directional test *provided that the outcome is in the direction stated in the* Alternative Hypothesis. But if the data show a difference in the opposite direction, then the same, or even a larger, difference will not be significant because it does not contradict the Null Hypothesis.

In order to use a directional test we must be able to predict the direction of the difference before collecting the data. And what is more, we are taking the view that any outcome in the direction opposite to the one predicted will be interpreted as a chance result *however great the effect turns out to be*. That is quite a strict requirement: would you *really* believe that a huge effect in the opposite direction must have been the result of chance – or instead would you be tempted to look for some other explanation? As a rule, it is better always to use a non-directional test unless you have a very good reason not to.

Before carrying out any significance test, it is best to formulate a Null Hypothesis and an Alternative Hypothesis and write these down. Ask yourself the following questions to guide your thinking.

Q: Can you write a sentence stating that the experimental effect you are interested in does not exist so any difference observed in your data is the result of chance alone?

That will constitute your Null Hypothesis.

Q: What is the exact opposite of your Null Hypothesis – a hypothesis that affirms everything that the Null Hypothesis denies?

That will constitute your Alternative Hypothesis.

Q: What explanations other than chance could account for what was observed?

If more than one explanation is available, the test of significance will not be able to tell you which is the true answer. Eliminating alternative explanations is the task of good experimental design.

Q: Do the non-chance explanations all predict the same direction of difference?

If they do, a directional test may be appropriate, but that is exceedingly rare in the behavioural sciences. If in doubt, use a non-directional test.

SAQ
3

Yesterday you noticed your cat leaving the house by the back door and returning through the front door and it occurred to you that she might prefer not to use the same door twice in succession. Since you had to be at home today you have taken careful note of her comings and goings. She has left the house 15 times and on only 4 occasions did she return through the same door.

(a) *Should a statistical test of the possibility that the cat prefers not to use the same door twice in succession be directional or non-directional?*

(b) *Write down a Null Hypothesis that could be tested to give evidence on the matter.*

(c) *Write down the Alternative Hypothesis corresponding to that Null Hypothesis.*

Summary

❑ Our information comes from samples but we generally want to know about populations. We can generalize from small samples to wider populations, but always with some uncertainty.

❑ The Null Hypothesis is a model in which chance is the only explanation needed to account for the observed results.

❑ Statistical tests calculate the probability of obtaining results such as those in our data and any that disagree even more with the Null Hypothesis.

❑ If the statistical test is significant (that is, if the resulting probability is small enough), we reject the Null Hypothesis and conclude that the results support the Alternative (or Experimental) Hypothesis.

❑ Type 1 errors occur when we mistakenly conclude that something other than chance is responsible for the results. Type 2 errors occur when we fail to conclude that anything other than chance is at work, even though there is some other, real influence on the results.

❑ Changing the probability that we consider 'significant' makes one type of error less likely but makes the other type more likely. The best level to choose depends on whether Type 1 or Type 2 errors are more objectionable.

❑ If a statistical test is not significant, we can not reject the Null Hypothesis, but we can not reach any other firm conclusion either.

❑ Directional tests are appropriate only if we are prepared to attribute to chance any effect (however large) in the direction opposite to the one indicated by the Experimental Hypothesis.

2 The characteristics of significance tests

KEY AIMS: By the end of Part 2 you should understand:
- ▷ *the three components of any test of significance;*
- ▷ *the need for statistical tables;*
- ▷ *the difference between distribution-free and distribution-dependent tests;*
- ▷ *considerations affecting the choice of a statistical test.*

If a recipe asks for a lump of dough the size of an orange and another the size of a tomato you can follow it okay, and the first lump will be larger. I expect you have a fair idea of the typical size of an orange and a tomato and you'll probably agree that an orange is much the same size as a tennis ball, even though there are lots of individual oranges that are larger or smaller than that. You probably agree too that a tomato is much the same size as a snooker ball. However, you are well aware that lots of tomatoes are larger than some small oranges so you would be somewhat uncertain what difference to expect between any *particular* samples of oranges and tomatoes.

Helen Welford

The same is not true of tennis balls and snooker balls! You can be quite sure that every tennis ball is bigger than every snooker ball, so in every sample of tennis balls and snooker balls the difference will be in the same direction. That is true even though the difference is about the same as that between oranges and tomatoes! Your greater certainty is not because the difference is greater but because the *variability* of the difference is *smaller*.

What makes us confident that a difference is a real one? For tennis balls and snooker balls, it is the high consistency of the differences we observe. To take the argument further, melons are just as variable in size as oranges, yet we have no doubt at all that melons are larger than tomatoes. In this case, it's the

© Copyright. No photocopying allowed

10

large *average difference* that makes us confident that melons are larger. Finally, how can we be sure that oranges are *generally* bigger than tomatoes even though there are so many exceptions? It is because we have encountered lots of examples of each. *The more data we accumulate, the more confident we become*, even if the results are rather variable.

There are many different ways to calculate statistical significance but they all have some features in common and it helps to have them in mind when learning a new method. All significance tests consist of a calculation involving:

> the size of a difference;
> the variability of that difference;
> the amount of data available.

Victoria: *Why are you so bothered by that noise? Your car's always making funny noises.*

Albert: *Yes, but this one's quite loud – and it's been there ever since that long run last week.*

The reason Albert, in this dialogue, is particularly worried about the car's new noise is that it is louder than most (a large effect) and has continued for some time (low variability and a lot of data). These lead him to think that it is not just one of the many, random 'funny noises' that his car is inclined to make.

Try to spot these three elements in the statistical formulae on the following pages. Each test calculates the probability of obtaining results by chance alone. That probability will be smaller (and the results are therefore more likely to be significant) if:

❑ **the difference is large**;

❑ **the variability is small**;

❑ **the amount of data is large**.

There is another factor that inclines Albert to take the car's 'funny noise' seriously: he suspects that it may have something to do with the long journey he made last week. This is not a factor that changes the strength of the evidence provided by the noise itself but, because it gives a reason for thinking that something *might* be wrong, its effect is to make him *willing to be convinced by weaker evidence* from the noise – that is, it makes him more willing to risk Type 1 errors.

In the same way, the level of significance that we find convincing in a particular experiment is influenced by the reasonableness of the Alternative Hypothesis. If the non-chance explanation is one that we are quite ready to accept, we will be persuaded by a significance level of 0.05. If the Alternative Hypothesis involves a conclusion that we think very unlikely, we are reluctant to believe it so a significance level of 0.05 may not be enough to persuade us to reject the Null Hypothesis. We want results that are significant at the 0.01 or 0.001 level before we are persuaded.

Using statistical tables

Significance tests involve calculating a single number, a **test statistic**, whose size depends on the size of the difference, the variability of the results and the amount of data. For each test statistic, mathematicians have worked out how likely we are to obtain any particular value by chance alone (that is, if the Null Hypothesis is true) and to save us working it out again we can consult their **statistical tables**. From the relevant table we can tell how large (or how small) a particular statistic must be in order to be significant at a particular level of probability. Statistical tables can be laid out in different ways so don't be confused if they look different in different books – they all lead to the same conclusions if they are used properly.

A note of caution: as we shall see, some statistical tests yield a test statistic for which *large* values are significant whereas others need a *small* value for a significant result. Don't worry about this. In practice, it is always easy to tell which way round it is for any particular statistic since it is always stated clearly in the heading to the table.

Look now at tables A to F at the end of this Unit. Exactly how the tables are used will be described later when we look at the tests they apply to. You will see they show the largest, or the smallest, value of the statistic that is significant. That is done both for the 0.05 and for the 0.01 levels of significance in a non-directional (two-tailed) test. We can reject the Null Hypothesis in favour of the Alternative Hypothesis if the table shows that the statistic we obtained is significant.

Statistical tests lead to aggregate conclusions. The various sorts of conclusion we draw for scientific purposes were discussed in Unit 1, *Models and Methods for the Behavioural Sciences*. In particular, we looked at **aggregate** and **general** conclusions. Now consider oranges and tomatoes. Our conclusion about their relative sizes is an aggregate conclusion because it is true only *on average*. The conclusion about tennis balls and snooker balls and the one about melons and tomatoes are **general** conclusions – they are true in every case. Remember: *conclusions that depend on statistical significance are always aggregate*. Anything that happens without exception hardly needs a statistical test to convince us.

SAQ
4

You have been trying to improve your basketball shooting by regular practice. The day you began your current training you got 20 balls in out of 50. Today, out of 50 shots you got 40 in. In case today's score was just luck you carried out a test of significance (a two-sample chi-squared test, described in Part 6). It tested the Null Hypothesis that any difference between today's score and the earlier score is attributable to luck alone and the result turned out to be significant at the 0.01 level.

(a)   *Should your Null Hypothesis be directional or non-directional?*
(b)   *Write down a suitable Null Hypothesis.*
(c)   *What conclusion should you draw from the significant result?*
(d)   *Is the conclusion aggregate or general?*

Parametric and non-parametric tests of significance

Tests are often classified as **parametric tests** or as **non-parametric tests**. The *t*-test (described later) is a parametric test and the **Wilcoxon test**, and the **Mann-Whitney test** are non-parametric. The other tests described here occur in various forms, of which some are parametric and some are not. The difference between parametric and non-parametric tests is a technical one that need not concern us, and in any case the terms are used in different ways by different people.

It is usual for parametric tests to assume that the random errors affecting the results have a particular distribution – often, though not necessarily, the normal distribution. Tests that make such assumptions are called **distribution dependent tests**. Non-parametric tests generally make no assumption about the distribution of errors, and so are **distribution-free.**

Some textbooks state that parametric tests are appropriate only for certain types of data or contain guides to show which tests ought to be used for data at nominal, ordinal or interval scales of measurement. (These scale types are discussed in detail in Unit 1 and Unit 2.) Such guides provide only a rough indication of what is appropriate and can be misleading because they do not pay attention to what each test actually tries to achieve.

Some go even further and *define* a test as parametric if it requires data that has been measured on an interval or ratio scale, and as non-parametric if it is suitable for data measured on an ordinal or nominal scale. Occasionally, one even sees an expression such as 'parametric data', which has no statistical meaning at all. As a matter of fact, a non-parametric test *is* likely to be more suitable than a parametric test when measurement is not on an interval or ratio scale, but that is not what makes the test non-parametric!

Confusion about the terms 'parametric' and 'non-parametric' is so widespread that it may be best to avoid them. 'Distribution-dependent' and 'distribution-free' are not exactly equivalent, but usually describe the distinction that is in mind. They are easier to grasp and are used more consistently so these terms will be used here.

Selecting a suitable statistical test

In this Unit, the description of each test indicates which features of the data it is sensitive to. That is your best guide to selecting which test to use. Rather than thinking only of scale type, it is useful also to consider the possibility of **outliers** and the danger that a given difference between scores has widely different meanings at different points on the scale.

Another factor to consider is that distribution-free tests use less of the information in the data – for example, by using the rank orders of scores rather than the scores themselves. That has disadvantages – but also has advantages.

One disadvantage is that, because they use less of the information, such tests can be slightly less efficient than the *t*-test at demonstrating real differences when they exist. In other words, Type 2 errors may be more likely. (The technical expression is that distribution-free tests usually have less **power** – that is, power to reject the Null Hypothesis when it should be rejected.)

One advantage is that they are less likely to be misled by a few results that are eccentric, for whatever reason. Another is that they do not need to assume, as the *t*-test does, that random error in the measurements has a Normal distribution. (Though when there is a substantial amount of data – say 30 pairs of scores – the *t*-test is not much affected by the distribution not being Normal.)

The main disadvantage of distribution-free tests is one that is of little concern at this stage. It is that they are less versatile for handling complicated problems. Since we are dealing here only with fairly simple types of data, that does not matter. For most data you are likely to meet, the benefits of distribution-free methods outweigh their disadvantages. That is especially so when the amount of data is small, because that is when a failure to meet the strict requirements of the *t*-test matters most.

Building blocks for *t*-tests

Because the *t*-tests described here have much in common with far more complicated analyses that you may need in the future, it pays to understand the elements they are built from. We need three statistical concepts: the **sum of squares (SS), degrees of freedom (df)** and the **standard error (SE)**. We will put them to use in Part 3 but let us make their acquaintance briefly now.

The sum of squares (SS). The term should really be 'the sum of squared **deviations'** because that describes it exactly. If we calculate the mean of a set of numbers and find how much each number differs from the mean, these are the deviations. If we then obtain the squares of the deviations, and add up these squares we have the sum of squared deviations, usually known as the 'sum of squares'. If we denote the set of scores by X, their mean by $\bar{X}$ and the number of scores by N, we can describe its calculation by the following formula:

$$SS = \Sigma (X - \bar{X})^2$$

Another way of calculating it, which gives exactly the same answer and is often more convenient, is:

$$SS = \Sigma X^2 - \frac{(\Sigma X)^2}{N}$$

Degrees of freedom (df). This term refers to how many values in a set of data can be changed without necessarily affecting the values around which variation is occurring. An example will make it clearer.

When we calculate a standard deviation, the individual deviations are measured *around the mean*. How many of the deviations can take different values without altering the mean? If the mean is not to alter, neither must the *total* of the scores. If the total is to remain the same, we are able to alter the values of all but one of the scores. So if there are N scores, N - 1 of them are free to vary irrespective of the values of the other scores, so there are N - 1 degrees of freedom. Think of trying to seat ten people in a room with ten chairs. The first nine to sit down have a choice, but the tenth has only one possible seat and no freedom to choose.

'I'll have a baked potato please'

Helen Welford

The standard error (SE). There is likely to be a random element in almost any data we obtain, and the SE is a measure that expresses the uncertainty we therefore have about the true value of something. It does this by taking account simultaneously of the variability of the results and the amount of data. We will use the standard error of the *mean* (though a standard error can be calculated for any statistic). The SE of the mean can be calculated by the following formula:

$$SE = \sqrt{\frac{SS}{dfN}}$$

That is, we divide the sum of squares by the degrees of freedom and by the number of scores and then find the square root of that result.

How these elements relate to the three components of all statistical tests

Clearly, the standard error (SE) is going to be larger if the variability (measured by the sum of squares) is *large* or if the amount of data (measured by the degrees of freedom and number of scores) is *small*. Remember that a large amount of variability or a small amount of data makes us uncertain about any result. Thus, to be confident about a result – for the result to be statistically significant – we want the standard error to be small. As we shall see later, a *t*-test involves comparing the size of the observed difference with its standard error.

How statistical tests in this Unit are organized

This Unit is organized differently from most statistics books you are likely to meet and for very good reasons. Many books attach great importance to the distinction between 'parametric' and 'non parametric' methods. Many of them determine the choice of test by the scale type of the measurements. That idea can be misleading and it is not used here. Instead, this Unit aims to give a better understanding of the underlying logic and a better preparation for applying them.

We look first at tests that can be used with scores or measurements (in Parts 3 and 4) and later at those used with frequencies – numbers of instances – (in Parts 5 and 6). Within each of these two groups, we look first at methods suitable for a single sample or two matched samples (in Parts 3 and 5). Next, we look at methods suitable for two independent samples (in Parts 4 and 6).

Summary
- All results are more significant when: the effect is large; the variability is small; there is a lot of data.
- Statistical tables are consulted to discover if the test statistic is large enough (or small enough) for the results to be significant.
- The terms 'parametric' and 'non parametric' are widely misunderstood and are better avoided if possible. The related terms 'distribution-dependent' and 'distribution-free' are preferable.
- It is generally advisable to use distribution-free tests when outliers are likely or when a particular numerical difference in scores means something different with pairs of small scores from what it means with pairs of large scores.
- The concepts: sum of squares (SS), degrees of freedom (df), and standard error (SE), are used in the *t*-test and also in tests that deal with more complex data than we consider here.

Inferences from scores that occur in pairs

KEY AIMS: By the end of Part 3 you should understand:
- ▷ *how to use the one-sample t-test;*
- ▷ *how to use the Wilcoxon test;*
- ▷ *how to use the sign test;*
- ▷ *when each of these tests should be preferred.*

Victoria: Their estimates were nearly all too long – are bus passengers really that pessimistic or were they just lucky that the bus came along early?

Albert: We need some way to work out the probability of getting estimates that far wrong.

In Unit 2 we looked at data from a small survey in which Victoria and Albert studied the expectations of bus passengers about how long they would have to wait and then timed the arrival of their buses. In general, passengers were pessimistic. Their estimates were mostly longer than the times they actually had to wait. But is that true of the local population of bus passengers – or could the pessimism of the sample have been just a matter of chance? Passengers varied widely in the accuracy of their estimates and maybe Victoria and Albert picked a sample whose errors just happened to be mainly in the same direction. We can use statistics to tell us how easily that can happen. Remember that the answer is going to depend on three things: the size of the difference, the variability of the data and the amount of data.

Here, we want to compare different scores obtained from the same individuals. We will use three significance tests: the **one-sample *t*-test** (also called the **related *t*-test**), the **Wilcoxon T test** and the **sign test**. With each of them, we will first investigate the difference between the estimated wait and the actual wait (the degree of pessimism if you like) for each of the 50 passengers in the survey. Later, we will use them for other purposes.

Q: All three tests can be used directionally or non-directionally. Should our Null Hypothesis be directional or non-directional in this case?

A: We should test a *non-directional* Null Hypothesis, since there is no logical reason why passengers should not give optimistic rather than pessimistic estimates.

Q: Can you say what is that Null Hypothesis?

A: It is that, on average, the waiting time estimated by a passenger is the same as the time taken by his or her bus to arrive.

It may seem that the Null Hypothesis is obviously wrong – after all, just by looking at the data we can see that most of the passengers gave estimates that were too long. But remember that a Null Hypothesis always concerns a population whereas our results describe only a sample. To generalize from one to the other we need a statistical test because it is perfectly possible that, *in the population*, estimates that are too long are balanced by others that are too short even

© Copyright. No photocopying allowed

if, in a sample from the same population, the two do not balance out exactly. A statistical test asks how plausible that explanation is.

Q: Given that our Null Hypothesis is that, on average, there is no difference between the times estimated by passengers and the times taken by the buses to arrive, what is the Alternative Hypothesis?

A: It is, of course, that, on average, there is *some difference* (in the population) between the times estimated by passengers and the times taken by the buses to arrive.

No direction for the difference is stated, even though we can see from the results that the estimates were too long, because there is no logical reason why passengers should not give underestimates. If that had been what the data showed, we would have been quite ready to believe it – we would not consider that it had to be a chance result. And remember, you state your Null and Alternative Hypotheses *before* collecting your data, not afterwards. Thus the Alternative Hypothesis is that there is *some difference*, but it does not specify what the difference is: it is a non-directional hypothesis.

One-sample *t*-test (related *t*-test)

The ***t*-test** is one of the most frequently-used statistical tests. Its **test statistic**, *t* can be calculated in various ways, though some of the different methods are only alternative calculations for obtaining the same result. All forms of *t*-test share the same basic approach, discussed in Part 2: some statistic is compared with its standard error. The method described here is used when the data consist of pairs of scores. Both members of each pair should be a score (or measurement) from a single individual or be related in some other way that justifies considering them as a pair.

We will now use a *t*-test to test the significance of the difference between the bus passengers' estimates and the times they each had to wait for their bus. The statistic that is relevant here is the mean difference between passengers' estimates and their actual waiting times. To obtain it, we calculate the difference, d, between these two scores for each person and then calculate the mean of all these differences. If they are purely a matter of chance, positive and negative differences will tend to cancel out, so the mean difference, $\bar{d}$, is likely to be near zero. If the mean difference is far from zero, it is one that is unlikely to arise if chance is its only cause – that is, we consider it to be statistically significant.

How large a difference needs to be before it is considered significant depends, as always, on the amount of data and its variability. The **standard error** is a measure which takes account of these factors, as we saw in Part 2. The SE is larger when there is less data or when variability is greater. We therefore *divide* $\bar{d}$ by the standard error of the mean difference, SE_d, to give the test statistic, *t*. That is:

$$t = \frac{\bar{d}}{SE_d}$$

Once we have found *t*, we can consult a statistical table to see if the result is significant. Let's do that for the results obtained by Albert and shown in Table 1.

TABLE 1. Results from 26 people in bus queues questioned by Albert.
The first column shows the passenger's estimate of how much longer it will be until the bus arrives. The second column is the number of minutes the passenger actually had to wait, so the first two columns contain the raw data. The third column shows the difference between the estimate and the actual wait and the fourth shows the square of that difference. Columns 3 and 4 are calculations from the raw data needed for our test of significance.

Passenger's Estimate	Passenger's Wait	Difference (d)	Squared Difference (d^2)
15	9	6	36
10	5	5	25
5	6	-1	1
15	8	7	49
20	8	12	144
5	4	1	1
10	7	3	9
2	3	-1	1
5	4	1	1
12	5	7	49
7	6	1	1
3	4	-1	1
5	3	2	4
8	7	1	1
20	9	11	121
15	12	3	9
13	8	5	25
15	11	4	16
11	8	3	9
5	2	3	9
5	7	-2	4
10	12	-2	4
15	7	8	64
30	3	27	729
10	11	-1	1
20	8	12	144
Totals		114	1458

$\Sigma d = $ 114 $\Sigma d^2 = $ 1458   N (Number of differences) = 26

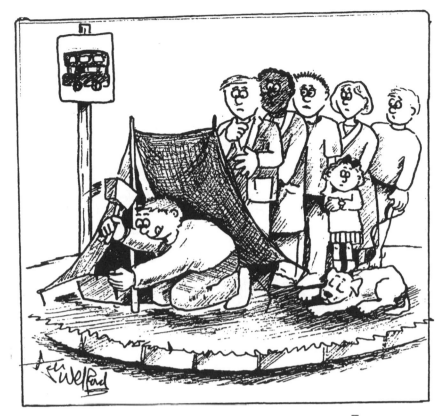

From these results we can calculate the mean difference ($\bar{d}$) and the sum of squares of the differences (SS_d), thus:

$$\bar{d} = \frac{\Sigma d}{N} = \frac{114}{26} = 4.385$$

$$SS_d = \Sigma d^2 - \frac{(\Sigma d)^2}{N} = 1458 - \frac{114^2}{26} = 958.154$$

We can now calculate the standard error of the differences (SE_d):

$$SE_d = \sqrt{\frac{SS_d}{df\,N}} = \sqrt{\frac{958.154}{25 \times 26}} = 1.214$$

We now calculate t by dividing $\bar{d}$ by SE_d:

$$t = \frac{\bar{d}}{SE_d} = \frac{4.385}{1.214} = 3.612$$

Positive and negative differences. It is essential that the differences are calculated in the same way for each passenger. For instance, in the above example we always subtracted the actual wait from the estimated wait, (though it would have been just as acceptable to subtract the estimated wait from the actual wait). Notice that the differences are negative when the estimate is less than the waiting time. In calculating the total to be 114, the negative numbers have partly cancelled out the positive ones. Don't worry if the total (and hence the mean) difference you get is negative. Negative results are just as much an indication of a difference as positive ones, so in all *subsequent* calculations it's okay to ignore the negative sign. When we speak of a *large value of t*, it means one that is a long way from zero, but quite possibly is negative.

Interpreting the _t_ we obtain. Large values of _t_ indicate a significant result. Why are large values of _t_ significant? Remember which factors decrease the probability of getting results by chance. Chance is an unlikely explanation for results where the variability (SS_d) is small or where the amount of data (N) is large.

In such cases, SE_d is small, since $SE_d = \dfrac{SS_d}{N}$.

The other factor making results significant is a large difference. Since $t = \dfrac{\bar{d}}{SE_d}$, _t_ becomes larger as the difference, $\bar{d}$, increases or its standard error, SE_d, decreases.

To discover whether or not the result is significant (and at what level) in a particular case, we must consult a table of _t_ – see Table A at the end of this Unit. Table A has columns corresponding to the two significance levels we are using (0.05, and 0.01) and rows corresponding to different numbers of degrees of freedom (df).

Degrees of freedom in a one-sample _t_-test

For many test statistics, including _t_, the value needed for a significant result depends on how many degrees of freedom there are. For the one-sample _t_-test, with N pairs of scores, and hence N differences, df = N - 1 – all the differences could be changed except for one without altering the total difference, Σd, that we use in the calculation.

Here there are 26 pairs, so df = 25. For the present results, _t_ is 3.612. To use Table A we would like to consult the row corresponding to df = 25 but we find that there is no such row. When that happens, we must consult the closest row with a _smaller_ number of df – the one where df = 24. In that row, within the column headed 0.05, we see a value of 2.064. That is the _minimum_ size _t_ must be if it is to meet the corresponding level of significance, $p \leq 0.05$, so we conclude that our result is significant at the 0.05 level. We can now be bolder and consider a higher level of significance (a smaller probability of Type 1 error), the 0.01 level. Our result is larger than that too (3.612 compared with 2.797 that the table tells us is needed) so we can conclude that the result is significant at the 0.01 level. (Note that it is pointless to report that the result is significant at _both_ the 0.05 and the 0.01 level: if it is significant at 0.01 it _must_ also be significant at 0.05.)

Drawing conclusions from significant results

Having concluded that the result is significant, the analysis is not yet over. We must say not only that it's significant but also what that tells us about the topic we are investigating. In this case, it tells us that the passengers made estimates of the time they would have to wait that were, on average, longer than the times that they then had to wait. Because the result was significant, we consider the result to be a real one – true of the population of all passengers using the bus service and not only of the sample questioned. Thus the answer to Victoria's question is that passengers, _in general_, really are pessimistic (on average, and with some exceptions, since the conclusion is only an aggregate one) – we have shown that the result is one that would rarely happen if that wasn't true.

However, after _every_ significance test we must keep at the back of our minds the thought that we might be mistaken. A result being significant at the 0.01 level implies that a Type 1 error will occur only one time in 100 if the Null Hypothesis is true. But if this is one of those few occasions – and it could be – our conclusion about the population is mistaken, though that's in no way our fault: it's an accidental consequence that can always affect this kind of inference.

Why bother then? Well, statistics are powerful tools, but with behavioural data there is no such thing as being one hundred percent sure. Investigators can only do their best by formulating hypotheses precisely, paying attention to the details of experimental design and then being careful to draw only those conclusions that the data really justify. A good way to report a significant result is to say:

> **The result is significant so we reject the Null Hypothesis that chance alone is responsible for the data.**

Having rejected mere chance as an explanation, we can then refer to the observed results and argue for any other explanation for the results that seems to be justified.

Even when things MIGHT BE equal we don't know that they ARE

What if the result is not significant? Suppose that instead of being greater than 2.064 (the value needed to reach the 0.05 significance level with 24 df) the *t* we calculated had been smaller than that – what should we conclude?

We should be careful not to draw any definite conclusion. The result is not significant, so we cannot reject the Null Hypothesis – chance is able to explain the results without any other factor being involved. On the other hand, the result certainly does not prove that chance *was* the only factor at work. Remember that to be confident of a result we require a large difference, a small variability and/or a large amount of data. One possible explanation for a result being non-significant is that any difference there may be is small compared with the variability. However, there is always another possibility: there may actually be an important difference but we have too little data to show it clearly. A good way to report such a result is to say:

> **The result is not significant, so we have insufficient evidence to reject the Null Hypothesis**.

In that way we make it clear that although we are not able to reject the Null Hypothesis we are not accepting it as the whole truth either.

SOMETHING TO TRY (Answer is at end of Unit)

Table 2 shows the results obtained when Victoria questioned passengers about how long they expected to wait and timed the arrival of the bus. Carry out a t-test to determine if the apparent pessimism shown by her passengers is significant.

TABLE 2. Results from 24 bus passengers questioned by Victoria.

The first column shows the passenger's *estimate* of how much longer it will be until the bus arrives. The second column is the number of minutes the passenger actually had to *wait*.

Passenger's Estimate	Passenger's Wait	Difference (d)	Squared Difference (d²)
4	2		
3	6		
15	6		
5	1		
4	2		
8	7		
10	7		
8	11		
5	3		
8	11		
6	11		
20	6		
10	7		
6	5		
1	4		
15	5		
5	3		
20	11		
12	8		
12	6		
5	2		
20	12		
20	6		
5	3		

Carrying out a one-sample t-test

Number of differences	N	$= 24$
Total of differences	Σd	$=$
Total of squared differences	Σd^2	$=$
Mean difference	$\bar{d}$	$=$
Sum of squares of the differences	SS_d	$=$
Standard error of the differences	SE_d	$=$
Test statistic	t	$=$
Degrees of freedom	df	$=$
Required size of t for significance at 0.05		$=$
Required size of t for significance at 0.01		$=$
Conclusion:		

Wilcoxon Test (T)

Sometimes people are doubtful about the appropriateness of the *t*-test. There may be various reasons, but for now let's just note that some of the estimates by bus passengers were suspected of being **outliers** – scores that do not belong with the others because they have a different origin. Perhaps very high estimates indicated anger about the bus service rather than being true *estimates* of waiting time. Outliers can have a large effect on the mean, and consequently may give a misleading value for *t*. That is one good reason for sometimes preferring a method that does not use means. We will now carry out one such test – the Wilcoxon – using the same data, and compare the results.

The **Wilcoxon matched-pairs, signed-ranks test** (to give its proper title) also begins by calculating all the differences. (Just as with the *t*-test, we must be careful to obtain them all in the same way, for instance, always subtracting a score in the second set from the corresponding score in the first set.)

Instead of next calculating their mean as in the *t*-test, the Wilcoxon test puts all the differences into rank order of absolute size, ignoring signs (that is, for example, scores of 17 *and* of -17 have higher ranks than one of 16). If any differences are exactly zero, the corresponding results are dropped from the analysis. A rank of 1 is given to the difference closest to zero, whether it is positive or negative; 2 is given to the next larger, and so on, always irrespective of whether the difference is positive or negative. If several differences are equal, they all get the mean of their several ranks.

TABLE 3. Differences between the time before the bus arrives and passengers' estimates of the time they will have to wait (Albert's data from Table 1), along with the ranks of these differences

Passenger's Estimate	Passenger's Wait	Difference	Rank of Difference
15	9	6	19.0
10	5	5	17.5
5	6	-1	4.5
15	8	7	20.5
20	8	12	24.5
5	4	1	4.5
10	7	3	13.5
2	3	-1	4.5
5	4	1	4.5
12	5	7	20.5
7	6	1	4.5
3	4	-1	4.5
5	3	2	10.0
8	7	1	4.5
20	9	11	23.0
15	12	3	13.5
13	8	5	17.5
15	11	4	16.0
11	8	3	13.5
5	2	3	13.5
5	7	-2	10.0
10	12	-2	10.0
15	7	8	22.0
30	3	27	26.0
10	11	-1	4.5
20	8	12	24.5

N (Number of differences) = 26

Table 3 contains the same results as Table 1 (estimates by passengers and the actual times each had to wait) but instead of the squares of the differences, it contains their ranks. For example, there were eight differences of 1 or -1. If these eight were not exactly equal they would have had ranks of 1, 2, 3, 4, 5, 6, 7 and 8, but since they were all equal they all get the average of these ranks, which is 4.5. And so on...

SAQ
5

Why do all the differences of 3 get ranks of 13.5?

The next stage is to determine which direction of difference occurred least often. Here, negative differences occurred only six times while there were 20 positive differences. We now add up all the ranks awarded to the *less frequent* type of difference. The result is the test statistic, T. (Note that it is written as a capital letter whereas the previous *t*-test statistic has a small, italic letter. Take care not to confuse them!)

The ranks awarded to negative differences were, in order of occurrence down the table, 4.5, 4.5,4.5, 10, 10, 4.5. The total of these is 38, so this is the value of T for the results in Table 3. More briefly, T = 38. We now need to decide if this result is significant or not, but first consider the following question.

If all the differences had been in the same direction, can you say what value T would have?

T would be zero since T is the total of the *smaller* number of ranks (in this case the smaller number is 0). If most of the differences are in the same direction, or if all the differences in one direction are small, then T will be small. T will be large if both totals are about equal – that is, if differences in the two directions more or less cancel out.

Thus T is large when the two sets of scores are very similar and T is small when they are very different, so a small T is a sign that there is a consistent difference in one direction or the other.

To summarize
- ❑ With the Wilcoxon T statistic, it is *small* values that are more likely to be significant. (Previously, with *t*, it was *large* values that were significant.)
- ❑ A significant value of Wilcoxon's T indicates that the two groups of scores are different, because it shows that the differences between them are mainly in one direction.

In order to decide if T is significant, we need to consult Table B at the end of this Unit. We look at the column corresponding to the significance level and across the row corresponding to N, the number of differences we have ranked (remembering that differences of zero are dropped from the analysis, so N may be smaller than the total number of differences).

For the data in Table 3 there are no differences of zero so no cases need to be omitted, thus N is 26 . We see from Table B that T must not exceed 98 if it is to be significant at 0.05 and must not exceed 75 to be significant at 0.01. The T we obtained is 38, which is *smaller* than either of these values so $p \leq 0.01$. This result agrees with what we found previously using the *t*-test and again leads us to the conclusion that the passengers' own estimates differed significantly from the times they actually had to wait. Because the result is significant we can generalize and consider it to be true of the population of all passengers using the bus service and not only of the sample questioned.

SOMETHING TO TRY (Answer is at end of Unit)

Carry out a Wilcoxon matched-pairs, signed-ranks test on Victoria's data in Table 2 and interpret the result.

'Sign test'

Helen Welford

Sign test

You will remember that the *t*-test used raw scores and the Wilcoxon test used ranks of the differences. But even the ranks of the differences may sometimes be misleading. For instance, we may not be confident that the difference of 4 between ranks of 1 and 5 means the same in psychological terms as the difference of 4 between ranks of 21 and 25. If so, a possibility is to use the sign test (and its calculation is the simplest of all).

Instead of taking account of how large each difference is (as is done in the *t*-test) or the rank order of positive and negative differences (as in the Wilcoxon), the sign test only takes account of *how many* differences are positive and how many are negative (that is, how many have each *sign*, + or -). As with the Wilcoxon, if a difference is zero, that case is dropped from the analysis.

Look back at Albert's data in Table 3. Of the 26 differences, 6 were negative and 20 were positive. The sign test uses only that information, without paying any attention to how big any of the differences were.

The *smaller* number is the test statistic, but it has no recognized symbol. Referring to Table C at the end of this Unit, look at the row corresponding to N, the number of differences used in the analysis (after we have dropped any which are zero). The number in the appropriate column shows the *largest* value the test statistic can have if it's to be significant. Consulting Table C, we find that for 0.01 significance and N = 26, the test statistic must be 6 or less. Thus the result is significant at the 0.01 level, in agreement with the previous results from the *t*-test and the Wilcoxon.

What if tests disagree?

Different tests applied to the same data set don't always agree as well as this. Sometimes we find that a result which the t-test or the Wilcoxon shows to be significant is not significant according to the sign test. That is quite okay. The reason is that the sign test uses less of the available information, so it is less sensitive. For example, it does not pay attention to the fact that the six negative differences in Table 3 are also among the smallest. Remember that a non-significant result *does not lead to any firm conclusion*, so it does not actually disagree with a significant result from another valid test. If you believe that any one of these three tests is valid, and it gives a significant result, that is evidence that something other than chance is at work in the data. If one of the tests is *not* significant, that does not prove that chance is the only explanation for the data. There is no contradiction: we believe the significant result, *provided that the requirements of the test are met*. That final point is now discussed further.

Which test should we use?

The t-test makes most use of the information contained in data by using the raw scores in its calculation, the Wilcoxon uses less of the information since it only pays attention to the ranks of the scores and the sign test uses least of all – only the direction of each difference. As a result, their power (that is, their ability to show that a particular difference is significant when it really does exist in the population) decreases in the order t-test (most power) to sign test (least power). That is a reason for preferring them in the order given, but it's not an overwhelming reason. By using more of the information, the t-test is more affected by outliers. It may also be somewhat questionable when measurement is not on an interval, ratio or absolute scale, because the meaning of a difference then varies from point to point on the scale. That problem is shared by the Wilcoxon too, though to a smaller degree. It does not apply to the sign test.

A further problem with the t-test is that it expects any random variation in scores to follow the normal distribution. That is often true, and in any case the lack of normality has to be extreme before it makes an important difference, but it is another argument often put forward for using one of the distribution-free methods such as the Wilcoxon or the sign test.

If there is a fair amount of data, say 30 or more pairs of scores, there is little danger in using the t-test unless inspection of the data suggests that there may be serious outliers. The less data we have, the stronger become the arguments for using the Wilcoxon, or even the sign test, if we want to guard carefully against Type 1 errors. As in most things, there is no perfect solution and we must settle for a compromise.

All of the tests described in this Part are for use with data consisting of *pairs of scores*. Pairs most often arise when each person in an investigation yields two numbers – the estimated and the actual waiting time of each passenger, for instance. Sometimes, scores are in pairs because participants have been matched in some way. For instance, each member of a control group may be selected to have the same age as someone in the experimental group. (They would then be referred to as an '*age-matched control group*'.) A score from a member of the control group and one from the member of the experimental group who has been matched in age in this way can then be treated as a pair. Matching of control participants to experimental participants always carries a risk of making the control group untypical in some other way, so matching is a procedure to be used with caution. However, if it is done, the analysis of the data can be carried out just as though the two scores in the pair had come

$SS_f = 194.92$

$\bar{x} = 3.071$

$SS_m = 114.90$

$\bar{M} = 5.90$

from a single individual, and one of the tests described in this Part can be used.

Ask yourself the following questions to help you decide which of these three tests, if any, to use.

Question	What does the answer tell you?
Are your results *pairs* of scores (measurements) with each pair relating to a single individual or to two individuals who have been matched in some way?	⇨ If yes, one of these tests will be appropriate. If no, none of them will be.
Do you think that means and standard deviations are appropriate measures to describe your results?	⇨ If yes, use the one-sample *t*-test.
Do you think medians and inter-quartile ranges are more suitable than means and standard deviations to describe your results?	⇨ If yes, use the Wilcoxon test or the sign test.
Do you suspect that your measurement scale has very unequal intervals or that there are serious outliers?	⇨ If yes, use the sign test rather than the Wilcoxon.

Summary
- ❑ Tests described in Part 3 are for use with *pairs* of scores: either two scores from each individual or one score from each of two individuals who have been matched in some way.
- ❑ The one-sample (or 'related') *t*-test uses the original scores. To be appropriate, the property on which the scores are being compared should be measured on an interval or ratio scale, the distribution of the differences should be approximately normal and there should be no outliers.
- ❑ These requirements are less strict if there is a substantial amount of data (say 30 pairs of scores).
- ❑ The Wilcoxon test is a little less powerful than the *t*-test but is less likely to give a misleading answer if the requirements of the *t*-test are not met.
- ❑ The sign test is less powerful than the Wilcoxon test but has even fewer requirements concerning the data.

4

Inferences from scores that are not in pairs

KEY AIMS: By the end of Part 4 you should understand:
▷ *how to use the two-sample t-test for unrelated scores;*
▷ *how to use the Mann-Whitney test for unrelated scores;*
▷ *when to use each of these tests.*

Victoria: The men's estimates were much worse than the women's!
Albert: But is the difference significant?

The comparisons in Part 3 all concerned differences between pairs of scores. Pairs of scores often come from one person or from two people who have been matched in some way. We are now going to look at ways of comparing scores that are not in pairs. We will compare the responses about the bus service from the female passengers with those from the male passengers, and there is no reason to relate the score of a female passenger to that of any particular male. We will try to decide if females are more or less pessimistic than males in their estimates of waiting time. Both of the tests we shall be using – the two-sample *t*-test and the Mann-Whitney test – can be used directionally or non-directionally.

Q: *Should our Null Hypothesis be directional or non-directional in this case?*
A: We should test a *non-directional* Null Hypothesis, since there is no logical reason why the scores of males should differ in any particular direction from those of females.

Can you say what that Null Hypothesis is? It is that, on average, there is no difference between the times estimated by male passengers and by female passengers. But is it really necessary to carry out a statistical test of this hypothesis? Can't we see at once, just by inspecting the data, that males gave longer estimates? Well, yes, we can but it *is* necessary to carry out a statistical test. The reason is that the results only tell us about the *sample* whereas we want to know about the *population* – is the difference true not just of those who were studied but of *all* such passengers?

Q: *What then is our Alternative Hypothesis?*
A: It is that, on average, there is *some difference* (in the population) between the times estimated by males and the times estimated by females. No direction for the difference is stated, even though we can see from the results that the males in the sample gave estimates that on average were longer than those of the females; but there is no logical reason why the results could not be the other way round. If the data had shown a difference in the opposite direction wouldn't we have been quite willing to believe it?

In comparing different scores for the same person, we began each time by calculating the difference between the scores. Here, there is no reason to compare a particular male's score with that of any particular female. This means that for scores like these, coming from different and unmatched individuals, we *must not* use the one-sample *t*-test, the Wilcoxon test or the sign test because all of these tests compare *corresponding pairs* of scores. When scores are not in pairs, we must use other statistics. Here, we will look at two tests: the **two-sample *t*-test** and

© Copyright. No photocopying allowed

the **Mann-Whitney test** and in Part 6 we will meet a third way of comparing two groups of scores, called the **Median test**.

Two-sample *t*-test

As one might expect, this version of the *t*-test evaluates the significance of the difference between the scores of two unrelated samples. Here, we are considering the difference between male and female bus passengers. We calculate a *t* statistic by dividing the difference we are interested in (that between the mean estimates of the males and of the females) by the standard error (SE) of that difference, just as in the one-sample *t*-test. That is:

$$t = \frac{\bar{X}_M - \bar{X}_F}{SE}$$

To make it clear which mean ($\bar{X}$), sum of squares (SS) number of individuals (N) and degrees of freedom (df) we are referring to, we will write them $\bar{X}_M$, $\bar{X}_F$, SS_M, SS_F, N_M, N_F, df_M and df_F to distinguish between males and females.

We obtain the sums of squares (SS) for males and for females in the same way as before, by squaring and adding the deviations from the mean. The only new element in this two-sample version of the *t*-test is the way that the standard error is calculated. We get it from the formula:

$$SE = \sqrt{\frac{SS_M + SS_F}{df_M + df_F} \left(\frac{1}{N_M} + \frac{1}{N_F}\right)}$$

Although the formula for the standard error is more complex than that for the one-sample *t*-test, it has the same elements. Can you see what these are? (Remember the three components that every test of significance depends on.)

We see that SE will be small if *the amount of data* (N_M, N_F, df_M, df_F, all in the bottom line of the equation) is large or if *the variability* of the results ($SS_M + SS_F$, in the top line) is small. We then obtain *t* by dividing the difference between the means ($\bar{X}_M - \bar{X}_F$) by the SE, thus:

$$t = \frac{\bar{X}_M - \bar{X}_F}{SE}$$

 If the SE is small or the difference between the means of the males and of the females ($\bar{X}_M - \bar{X}_F$) is large, then *t* will be large. As with the one-sample *t*-test, we need a large value for *t* to be significant though it will not matter whether *t* is a positive or a negative number: that depends only on which mean is subtracted from the other and not on the size of the difference between them. We ignore the sign and always treat the answer as positive.

Male and female bus passengers: are their estimates different?

So far we have paid no attention to the gender of any passenger, but in fact the first 14 of Albert's passengers in Table 1 were female and the remaining 12 were male. In Table 4, these results are split into two columns so they can be compared more easily. The first two columns of Table 4 show their estimates of waiting time. From the column totals we can calculate means, and we see at once that the males gave estimates that were, on average, longer.

The second two columns contain the squares of these estimates. We will use these figures to examine the possibility of a difference in the sorts of estimate given by males and females. The Null Hypothesis we will test is:

The mean estimates of males do not differ from the mean estimates of females.

TABLE 4. Estimates of the time they expect to wait given by 14 female and 12 male passengers interviewed by Albert

Females (F)	Males (M)	F^2	M^2
15	20	225	400
10	15	100	225
5	13	25	169
15	15	225	225
20	11	400	121
5	5	25	25
10	5	100	25
2	10	4	100
5	15	25	225
12	30	144	900
7	10	49	100
3	20	9	400
5		25	
8		64	
Totals 122	169	1420	2915

From these results we can now calculate a two-sample t-test.

For Females

$$\bar{F} = \frac{\Sigma F}{N_F}$$

$$= \frac{122}{14}$$

$$= 8.714$$

$$SS_F = \Sigma F^2 - \frac{(\Sigma F)^2}{N_F}$$

$$= 1420 - \frac{122 \times 122}{14}$$

$$= 356.857$$

For Males

$$\bar{M} = \frac{\Sigma M}{N_M}$$

$$= \frac{169}{12}$$

$$= 14.083$$

$$SS_M = \Sigma M^2 - \frac{(\Sigma M)^2}{N_M}$$

$$= 2915 - \frac{169 \times 169}{12}$$

$$= 534.917$$

$$SE = \sqrt{\frac{SS_F + SS_M}{df_F + df_M} \left(\frac{1}{N_F} + \frac{1}{N_M}\right)}$$

$$SE = \sqrt{\frac{356.857 + 534.917}{13 + 11} \left(\frac{1}{14} + \frac{1}{12}\right)}$$

$$SE = 2.398$$

$$t = \frac{\bar{F} - \bar{M}}{SE}$$

$$t = \frac{8.714 - 14.083}{2.398}$$

$$t = -2.239$$

We see that t is -2.239. Do not be concerned that t has a negative value. It is negative only because we subtracted the mean score of the males from the mean score of the females and we might equally well have subtracted the mean of the females from the mean of the males. That would have produced a positive number. In all *subsequent* calculations we can consider t as positive.

To discover if it's significant we use Table A. The df in a two-sample t-test comparing groups with N_1 and N_2 scores is N_1-1 + N_2-1, that is, in this case, 13 + 11, or 24, the sum of the df of the two groups of scores. In the row for 24 df we see that for significance at the 0.01 level, t must be at least 2.797 so the result is not significant at the 0.01 level. But we see that to be significant at the 0.05 level, t needs to be 2.064 or greater and the t we obtained exceeds that, so $p \leq 0.05$.

Interpreting a significant result

Our conclusion is that, on average, males give longer estimates of the time they expect to wait than females do (because $\bar{X}_M$ is larger than $\bar{X}_F$). Because the difference is significant, we conclude that the difference is true not only for our samples but also for the general population of passengers from which these samples of males and females were drawn.

We can now speculate as to why such a difference might occur. There are at least two possible explanations: (1) males may be inclined to give longer estimates of waiting time, whatever the true circumstances; (2) males who were sampled really did have longer to wait than the females and their estimates just reflected that difference. The analysis we have completed does not allow us to distinguish between these possibilities, but we could investigate the data further in order to do so.

What if t had not been significant?

Note that the conclusion from a non-significant result is *not* that there is no difference between the groups studied (we can see there was a difference) and it is *not* that there is no difference between the populations they came from! It is that the difference observed is one that is quite likely to occur, *even if* there is no difference between the populations. However, if we are not able to reject the Null Hypothesis that chance alone can explain a result, we should not speculate about other reasons for any difference we observe. When reporting the result we can use a phrase like the one suggested in Part 3:

The result is not significant so we have insufficient evidence to reject the Null Hypothesis that there is no difference between the population means.

SOMETHING TO TRY (Answer is at end of Unit)

We found that males gave significantly longer estimates of waiting time — but was that because, on average, males are more pessimistic about their likely waits or because they really had longer to wait? (That might happen if they were less familiar with the bus timetables and so couldn't judge arrival times accurately, or if they were mostly waiting for the less frequent buses.)

If, instead of considering their estimates, we consider the errors in estimation by the male and by the female passengers we can test this. If errors are significantly greater for males, they are more pessimistic rather than having longer actual waits. Table 5 shows the errors — the difference between expected and actual waiting times — for the 26 passengers in Table 1. Use a t-test to compare the errors (shown in Table 5) of the male and the female passengers. Decide if they differ significantly and interpret the outcome.

TABLE 5. Errors by 14 female and 12 male passengers in estimating the time they expect to wait. An entry of 6 indicates that the passenger gave an estimate that was greater by 6 minutes than the time she actually had to wait. An entry of -1 indicates that the estimate was shorter by 1 minute than the actual wait.

Females (F)	Males (M)	F^2	M^2
6	11		
5	3		
-1	5		
7	4		
12	3		
1	3		
3	-2		
-1	-2		
1	8		
7	27		
1	-1		
-1	12		
2			
1			
Totals 43	71		

A word of caution. We may have doubts about using the two-sample t-test for the same reasons as for the one-sample t-test: the possibility of outliers distorting the results and the possibility that the distribution of scores is not normal. There is a further possibility in the two-sample case that the samples may be drawn from populations that have very different variabilities (and thus very different standard deviations). That too can give rise to misleading results with the simple form of t-test shown here. If any of these problems are suspected, the Mann-Whitney test may be preferred because it is less sensitive to them.

Mann-Whitney (U) test

The Mann-Whitney test uses a statistic called U. To calculate it, begin by ranking all the scores from the two samples just as though they were all one sample. The smallest score gets a rank of 1, the next a rank of 2, and so on, and equal scores get the average of their ranks.

Rank ordering

You can see immediately that if the scores in one sample are all smaller than those in the other, their ranks will be smaller too. If the scores are about the same size in each sample, the total ranks will be about equal in the two samples. Table 6 shows the estimates of female and male passengers, together with their ranks.

TABLE 6. Estimates by 14 female and 12 male passengers of the time they expect to wait, along with the ranks of these estimates

Estimates		Ranks	
Females (F)	Males (M)	Females	Males
15	20	20.0	24.0
10	15	12.5	20.0
5	13	5.5	17.0
15	15	20.0	20.0
20	11	24.0	15.0
5	5	5.5	5.5
10	5	12.5	5.5
2	10	1.0	12.5
5	15	5.5	20.0
12	30	16.0	26.0
7	10	9.0	12.5
3	20	2.0	24.0
5		5.5	
8		10.0	
Totals		149.0	202.0

The total of the ranks for the 14 females is 149 and for the 12 males it is 202 (though if we really want to save effort we need calculate only one of the totals). Now we can calculate U.

Let's call the numbers of cases in the two groups N_1 and N_2 and the sums of the ranks for the corresponding groups R_1 and R_2. We begin calculating the U statistic by summing the ranks given to the sample whose scores seem to be larger. If you aren't sure which is going to be larger, it doesn't matter – sum the ranks for either group because we can find U from either of them.

$$U = N_1 N_2 + \frac{N_1 (N_1 + 1)}{2} - R_1$$

We must now check that the value of U was calculated from the right group (the one whose scores are larger). We can do that by subtracting U from $N_1 N_2$, that is, by multiplying together the numbers of scores in the two groups and subtracting U from the answer. If the difference is *bigger* than U, we have calculated U correctly. If the difference is *smaller*, then the correct value for U is that difference. (That is why it does not really matter which sum of ranks is used – we come to the right answer by this stage anyway!) We will then need to consult suitable tables to discover if the calculated value of U is significant.

Let's see how all that works out in practice. Just to show that both sums of ranks lead to the same answer in the end, we will calculate U first from the totals of the males and then from that of the females. Of course we do not use both of them as a rule, since both methods give the same answer. For the males:

$$U_M = N_M N_F + \frac{N_M(N_M + 1)}{2} - R_M$$

$$= 12 \times 14 + \frac{12 \times 13}{2} - 202$$

$$= 168 + 78 - 202 = 44$$

To decide if we have the correct value of U we subtract 44 from 12x14, getting the answer 124. Since this is larger than 44, the correct value of U is 44. Now let's try it using the sum of ranks from the sample of females:

$$U_F = N_M N_F + \frac{N_F(N_F + 1)}{2} - R_F$$

$$= 12 \times 14 + \frac{14 \times 15}{2} - 149$$

$$= 168 + 105 - 149 = 124$$

To check if 124 is the correct value for U, we subtract it from 12x14, giving 44. Since that is smaller than 124, we know that the correct value for U is 44 – the same answer as we obtained using the other sum of ranks.

To discover if U is significant, we first consult Table E, examining the column corresponding to the number of cases in one of the samples and the row corresponding to the number of cases in the other. (It does not matter which is the row and which the column.) If U is *equal to or less than* the number in that cell of the Table, then the result is significant at the 0.01 level with a non-directional Null Hypothesis. Thus for the U statistic, it is *small* values that are significant. If the result is not significant at the 0.01 level, it might still be significant at the 0.05 level. To see if it is, we can go on to check Table D in the same way.

We see from Table E that for the difference between the groups to be significant at the 0.01 level, U must be 34 or smaller. For the results in Table 6, U is in fact 44 so the result is *not significant* at the 0.01 level. We now check Table D, where we find that to be significant at the 0.05 level, U must be 45 or smaller. Since the U we obtained is smaller than that, the result is significant at the 0.05 level.

Interpreting a significant result. As always, finding that a result is significant is not the end of the story. We must go on to say what the significant result actually means. What *does* it mean? We can see from the data that males had more large ranks (large estimates of waiting time), so we can conclude that males were significantly more likely than females to give long estimates. This result agrees with the conclusion we reached earlier in this Part by carrying out a two-sample *t*-test – males give longer estimates of waiting time. Like the *t*-test, however, it does not cast any light on *why* that occurs.

What if our groups are too large for Tables D and E?

If there's a lot of data, the arguments against using a *t*-test are weaker but, to be doubly safe, people often prefer a Mann-Whitney test even with large amounts of data. If we prefer to use a Mann-Whitney but have more scores than Tables D and E can cope with, we must carry the calculation a little further.

For a large amount of data, the mean value of U for two groups drawn from the same population is $\frac{N_1 N_2}{2}$ and its standard deviation is $\sqrt{\frac{N_1 N_2(N_1 + N_2 + 1)}{12}}$

By making use of these items of information, we can calculate a **standard score** (z-score) for any particular U, using this formula:

$$z = \frac{\dfrac{N_1 N_2}{2} - U}{\sqrt{\dfrac{N_1 N_2 (N_1 + N_2 + 1)}{12}}}$$

The formula yields a standard score (a deviation divided by the standard deviation) because the part above the line is the *deviation* of U from its mean and the part below is the standard deviation of U. The properties of standard scores were described in Unit 2, *Describing and Interpreting Data*, and you will remember that for scores that follow a normal distribution, we can use tables to tell us how likely any particular z is to be exceeded.

When N_1 and N_2 are large, the distribution of U is approximately Normal, so we can use tables of the Normal Curve. However, there is an even easier way to decide if the z we obtain is significant – it is the same as the t statistic with infinite (∞) degrees of freedom. (That is, the distribution of t is Normal when it is based on infinite degrees of freedom.) The values of z required to reach the 0.05 and 0.01 levels of significance are therefore those in the bottom row of Table A. From Table A we can see that z must be at least 1.960 to be significant at the 0.05 level and at least 2.576 to be significant at the 0.01 level in a non-directional test.

An example using the z calculation

Although Tables D and E contain rows and columns for groups of 12 and 14, let us nevertheless see how we would have used the z statistic to decide if the U of 44 we obtained from Table 6 is significant.

$$z = \frac{\dfrac{12 \times 14}{2} - 44}{\sqrt{\dfrac{12 \times 14 \times (12 + 14 + 1)}{12}}}$$

$$= \frac{84 - 44}{\sqrt{378}} = 2.057$$

The z we calculated from the U of 44 was 2.057, so this calculation tells us that the result is not significant at the 0.01 level (z is less than 2.576) but is significant at the 0.05 level (z is greater than 1.960). This agrees with the result we read from Tables D and E, even though the answer given by calculating z is only approximate. The approximation becomes even better as the amount of data increases – so for groups that are too large to allow Tables D and E to be used, the answer given by using z is quite satisfactory.

SOMETHING TO TRY (Answer is at end of Unit)

Participants in an investigation of attitudes to road accidents were shown a film of 10 incidents showing near accidents between motor vehicles and pedestrians. Each participant was asked to write down a score, on a scale from 0 to 10, for each incident to indicate how much blame for the incident was attributable to the pedestrian. The total score (0 to 100) allocated by each participant over the 10 incidents is shown in Table 7. The 9 participants who held a driving licence were classified as 'drivers' and the 7 who did not were classified as 'non-drivers'.

Carry out a Mann-Whitney test to decide if the scores allocated by the drivers differed significantly from those allocated by the non-drivers and interpret the outcome.

TABLE 7. Scores allocated by 9 drivers and 7 non-drivers to indicate the amount of blame attaching to pedestrians for 10 near-accidents in a film

Drivers	24	51	36	82	76	65	29	67	43
Non-drivers	23	66	35	12	11	28	32		

Summary

❑ Tests described in Part 4 are for use with two independent and unrelated groups of scores. The numbers of scores can be different in the two groups.

❑ The two-sample (or 'independent') t-test uses the original scores. To be appropriate, the measurements should be on an interval or ratio scale, the distribution within each group of scores should be approximately normal, and there should be no outliers in the data. The two sets of scores should have approximately the same standard deviation.

❑ The Mann-Whitney U test can be a little less powerful than the t-test but is less likely to give a misleading answer if these requirements are not met.

❑ If there is too much data to use Tables D and E of the Mann-Whitney U statistic, it is possible to discover the significance of the result by calculating a standard score, z, from U and referring to a table of t, for infinite degrees of freedom (a normal distribution).

Interpreting the frequencies of categories in a single sample

KEY AIMS: By the end of Part 5 you should understand:
▷ *how to use the chi-squared statistic to test the significance of a difference between observed and expected frequencies;*
▷ *what is meant by 'degrees of freedom' in a chi-squared test;*
▷ *how, and when, to use Yates's correction for continuity;*
▷ *how to carry out a sign test when the frequencies are too large for Table C.*

You have been waiting in a railway station for a friend whose train is late, and you've noticed something odd about the way people use the entrance. It consists of a row of five identical glass doors, but they have not been used equally often. There's no obvious reason why it should be so, but your data seem quite persuasive: some doors were used twice or three times as often as others. Let's identify the five doors by the letters A to E. The numbers of people using each door while you have been counting are shown in Table 8.

TABLE 8. Numbers of people using each of five doors in a railway station entrance

Door	A	B	C	D	E	Total
Number of users	7	15	5	10	5	42

Have you discovered an interesting fact about the way that everyone uses these doors? Not necessarily. Perhaps the doors are used about equally often in the long run – but just happened to have rather uneven use in the sample of 42 that you observed. A statistic called **chi-squared** can help us decide if that could reasonably be so.

Chi-squared compares **observed frequencies** (O), with **expected frequencies** (E). Its symbol is χ^2 (the Greek letter chi, squared) and the formula is:

$$\chi^2 = \Sigma \frac{(O-E)^2}{E}$$

O is a frequency that was actually observed (which in this case is the number of times a particular door was used) and E is the corresponding 'expected' frequency (which in this case is the number of times the door would be used if the doors are used equally often). The word 'expected' is in quotation marks because it is expected only in a mathematical sense and may not even be a *possible* frequency! (Frequencies must always be whole numbers but an expected frequency is a sort of average and is often not a whole number.) Σ is the usual instruction to add up the values that follow. (In this case, repeating the calculation for each of the five doors and adding the results.)

To be more precise, the symbol E refers to the average frequency we expect to observe if the Null Hypothesis is exactly correct. But what is the Null Hypothesis here? This is a general rule when we intend to calculate χ^2 from a table of frequencies:

© Copyright. No photocopying allowed

37

> **The Null Hypothesis makes a statement about *the probability* of each category.**

The usual Null Hypothesis is that all the probabilities are equal, but other Null Hypotheses are possible, as we shall see later. Since on this occasion we are considering the possibility that the doors are all used equally often, on average, our Null Hypothesis is: *All the doors have the same probability of being used.*

From our Null Hypothesis we can work out the expected frequencies. Once we have done that we can calculate χ^2, which will tell us if the observed frequencies differ *significantly* from the expected frequencies. If they do, we can conclude that the Null Hypothesis does not give a reasonable explanation of what was observed.

So how, exactly, do we calculate the expected frequencies? First, note that when we consider all five doors, the total of their probabilities must be 1.0 (since each individual in the data used one or other of the doors). If all five have an equal probability of being used, each probability must be 1/5, or 0.2. We can therefore calculate that the expected frequency for each door is 8.4 – that is, 42/5 or 42 x 0.2.

A rule to bear in mind that gives a way of checking the expected frequencies is this:

> **The total of the expected frequencies must be the same as the total of the observed frequencies.**

TABLE 9. Observed frequencies of using five doors by a sample of 42 people, and the expected frequencies that follow from the Null Hypothesis that all doors have an equal probability of being used

Door	A	B	C	D	E	Total
Observed	7	15	5	10	5	42
Expected	8.4	8.4	8.4	8.4	8.4	42

Notice that the expected frequencies in this case are not whole numbers. Observed frequencies must *always* be whole numbers.

Observed and expected frequencies

The calculation uses the formula for χ^2, making use of the observed and the expected frequency of using door A, door B and so on. It goes like this:

$$\chi^2 = \frac{(7 - 8.4)^2}{8.4} + \frac{(15 - 8.4)^2}{8.4} + \frac{(5 - 8.4)^2}{8.4} + \frac{(10 - 8.4)^2}{8.4} + \frac{(5 - 8.4)^2}{8.4}$$

$$= 0.233 + 5.186 + 1.376 + 0.305 + 1.376$$

$$\chi^2 = 8.476$$

Degrees of freedom in chi-squared

To discover if the resulting χ^2 of 8.476 is significant we will consult Table F at the end of this Unit, but to use it we need to know the number of degrees of freedom (df) in the calculation. We met degrees of freedom before in connection with the t-test. In the t-test, df were the number of scores free to vary about the mean. In chi-squared, it is the number of *observed frequencies* that are free to vary around the *expected frequencies*. Let's see what that amounts to in the present example.

We obtained the expected frequencies by multiplying the sample total (42) by the probabilities (0.2) given by the Null Hypothesis. Now these *probabilities* did not depend in any way on the data. They followed from the Null Hypothesis alone. But the *expected frequencies* we calculated did depend on the data in one respect: they depended on the *total* number of people (42) in the sample. If the sample had a different total, the expected frequencies for each door would not be 8.4 but one fifth of the new total. So, if the expected frequencies are to be 8.4 when testing that particular Null Hypothesis, the total of the observed frequencies must be 42.

The total can be 42 even if some of the observed frequencies change, but once we know the values of four observed frequencies, the remaining frequency must have some *particular* value to make the total 42. If the sample has 42 people and we find that the frequencies of using four of the doors are: 9, 4, 12, and 6, we have accounted for 31 people, so we know that exactly 11 must have used the remaining door. One of the five observed frequencies is not free to change independently. Thus, for the χ^2 we calculated there are 4 df.

Rules for degrees of freedom

You can generalize from this example to say that, when chi-squared is calculated in exactly this way from a sample divided into K categories, the number of df is equal to K-1. However, this rule does not express *what is meant by* the expression, 'degrees of freedom', and in some unusual cases it does not give the correct answer. The best way to think about degrees of freedom in χ^2 is to remember that:

> **df always equals the number of observed frequencies that could be different without changing any expected frequencies.**

This is a rule that works even for complicated applications of chi-squared where the simple 'K - 1' rule doesn't.

Note that the number of df depends only on the number of *categories*, and not on the number of *cases* in your data. In this example, df depends on the number of doors but not on the number of people using them.

What does the χ^2 result mean? We see from Table F that with 4 df, χ^2 must be 9.49 or greater to be significant at the 0.05 level. The result we have (8.476) is less than that, so it is not significant even at the 0.05 level. Since we cannot reject the Null Hypothesis, we conclude that the evidence is *not* sufficient to persuade us that the doors have different probabilities of being used. Frequencies of use as different as those that were observed will occur more than one time in 20 *even if all five doors have equal probabilities of being used.*

Remember that the data originally looked quite striking, with doors B and D being used much more often than doors C and E. But the analysis shows us that results like these, and others departing even further from equal frequency of usage, can actually occur fairly easily – or, at the very least, on more than one occasion in 20 – by chance alone, without there being any tendency in the population to prefer one door to another.

The numbers of male and female bus passengers

Victoria: *Lots more women were using the buses.*
Albert: *Maybe that was because of the times we were there.*

Let's think about the question Victoria and Albert are discussing: the numbers of male and female passengers in their sample. This topic can be tackled by a similar chi-squared calculation. There is one sample (50 passengers) divided into two categories, male and female. Although it looks simpler than the example involving five doors, an extra complication arises because there are only two categories rather than five!

The observed frequencies were 32 (female) and 18 (male). If the population of passengers contains equal numbers of males and females, the probability of a male being included in the survey sample is the same as the probability of including a female. To test if the observed frequencies depart significantly from that, we adopt the Null Hypothesis that: *The probabilities of male and female passengers being in the sample are equal.*

Note that this is a non-directional hypothesis and our Alternative Hypothesis is merely that the probabilities *are different.* Even though we found more females in our sample, we have no logical grounds to argue that the population of bus passengers *couldn't* contain more males than females.

Since a passenger must be either male or female, the total of these probabilities is 1.0, and if the two probabilities are equal, both must be 0.5. The 'expected' frequencies are obtained by multiplying the number in the sample (50) by the probability of each type of passenger, thus we obtain expected frequencies of $50 \times 0.5 = 25$ for both male and female passengers. We can check our calculation by making sure that the total of the expected frequencies is equal to the total of the observed frequencies. We can set out the results in two tables:

TABLE 10. Observed and expected frequencies of female and male bus passengers

Observed frequencies			Expected frequencies		
Female	Male	Total	Female	Male	Total
32	18	50	25	25	50

The expected frequencies follow from (a) the size of the sample, and (b) the particular Null Hypothesis we are testing. If we know the total number of people in the sample, then as soon as we learn what one frequency is, the other is known too. This χ^2, therefore, has just 1 df. A special formula is sometimes used for χ^2 when there is just one degree of freedom.

Yates's correction for continuity

When there is only 1 df, χ^2 is sometimes calculated in a slightly different way, for which the formula is:

$$\chi^2 = \Sigma \frac{(\,|O - E| - 0.5\,)^2}{E}$$

The pair of symbols | | are an instruction to make the number between them positive. For example, $2 - 5 = -3$ but $|2 - 5| = 3$.

What the formula means is that, as before, we find the difference between each observed frequency and its corresponding expected frequency, but now instead of just squaring the difference we first turn it into a positive number and subtract 0.5 from it. Only after that do we square it and divide by the expected frequency, E. This adjustment to the calculation is called **Yates's correction for continuity**.

The effect of the change is to make χ^2 smaller than it would otherwise have been. As a result, bigger departures of the observed from the expected frequencies are required before χ^2 becomes significant, so it reduces Type 1 error (which is more objectionable than Type 2 error in scientific work). Because of that, some people prefer to play safe and use it, even though many statisticians believe that the adjustment it makes to χ^2 is usually too great. But *remember not to use it unless there is just 1 df.*

Let's now calculate χ^2 from the results in Table 10 using Yates's correction.

$$\chi^2 = \frac{(\,|32 - 25| - 0.5)^2}{25} + \frac{(\,|18 - 25| - 0.5)^2}{25}$$

$$= \frac{42.25}{25} + \frac{42.25}{25}$$

$$\chi^2 = 1.69 + 1.69 = 3.38$$

What does this χ^2 tell us? Consulting Table F, we see that χ^2 needs to be 3.84 *or larger* for the result to be significant at the 0.05 level with 1 df. Since χ^2 is only 3.38, the result is *not significant*. As a result, we can't reject the Null Hypothesis that the probabilities of questioning a female and a male are equal. This is not to conclude that the probabilities are equal, it is just that they *reasonably could be* equal. (Remember that a non-significant result does not let us draw any definite conclusion.)

What the outcome of the chi-squared test really means is that if we take a sample completely at random from a population with equal numbers of females and males we will draw samples with proportions *at least as different as* 32:18 (such as 33:17, 34:16, 35:15 and also 18:32, 17:37, 16:34, and so on) on more than one occasion in twenty. Thus the sample obtained by Victoria and Albert is not a very unlikely one in respect of its numbers of males and females and gives us no strong grounds for believing that passengers using the service are more likely to be of one gender than the other.

Explaining a significant outcome

In the dialogue on p.40, Albert suggested that the reason they had more females than males in their sample might have been because of the times at which they conducted the survey. It's certainly possible that the proportion of male and female passengers varies from time to time throughout the day. Women are more likely to go shopping between 9 and 5, for example. Unless Victoria and Albert took particular care to conduct their survey at times chosen to cover the full day, it's quite possible that any difference they find will be biased and not typical. To prevent that possibility they would need to conduct a much more elaborate survey than they had time for.

Even if the chi-squared test had shown that the numbers of men and women in the sample were significantly different, it would not have told us why that was so. There are at least three possible reasons for the numbers being different and we could not have said which was the main one. There may be unequal numbers of men and women in the local population of bus passengers; there may be equal numbers in the population but unequal numbers at the particular times when the survey was conducted; finally, the numbers of men and women may have been equal at these times but Albert and Victoria did not sample them at random. It's possible too that *all* of these explanations contribute to the result. But similar problems apply to *every other inference we make* from the results of the survey. There are *always* possible explanations for results that can't be eliminated by statistical analysis but only by the way that a study is designed and carried out.

If the result had been significant at the 0.05 level, the proper conclusion would have been: *The χ^2 we obtained is significant at the 0.05 level so we conclude that numbers of males and females as unequal as those in the results are unlikely to arise if chance is the only cause. We therefore conclude that some factor other than chance affected the numbers of males and females occurring in the sample.* It is then open to us to speculate about what that non-chance 'something' may have been.

For the non-significant result that we actually obtained, the proper conclusion is: *The χ^2 we obtained is not significant at the 0.05 level so we conclude that a difference as great as the one we obtained, or greater, in the frequencies of male and female passengers, could reasonably occur by chance alone.* If we come to that conclusion, we should not seek any further explanation for the results.

"There's another possibility. Maybe he just doesn't like bananas"

SAQ
6

While writing an article about a proposal to build a new supermarket in the area, a reporter asked a sample of local shoppers if they were in favour of the plan or opposed to it. Thirty were in favour and ten were against it.

a) *What are the expected frequencies if local opinion is evenly divided about the topic?*
b) *How many df are there in a χ^2 calculated from these observed and expected frequencies?*
c) *Using Yates's correction for continuity, χ^2 is 9.025. What conclusions can be drawn about opinions regarding the proposed supermarket?*

The Null Hypothesis need not be that all probabilities are equal

The bus company knows from a large-scale survey it carried out previously that 55% of its passengers are male. Does Albert and Victoria's sample differ significantly from that in its proportion of male and female passengers? Again, we can calculate χ^2 to find out. The Null Hypothesis here is: *The probabilities of sampling male and female passengers are 0.55 and 0.45 respectively.*

Here, we have adopted as our Null Hypothesis the probabilities of a passenger being male or female that were found in the bus company's large survey. That is a sensible thing to do, since if a majority of passengers are known to be male it is reasonable to expect a random sample of passengers to reflect that fact.

The expected frequencies that follow from this Null Hypothesis are that 50 x 0.45 (= 22.5) of the sample are female and 50 x 0.55 (= 27.5) are male. If we know the total, then as soon as we discover one frequency, the other is known too. This χ^2, therefore, has just 1 df, so we will use Yates's correction for continuity in the calculation.

TABLE 11. Observed frequencies of female and male bus passengers in a sample of 50 and the expected frequencies that follow from the Null Hypothesis that the probabilities of sampling male and female passengers are the same as in an earlier survey

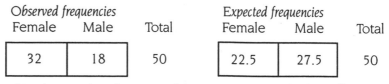

| Observed frequencies | | | Expected frequencies | | |
Female	Male	Total	Female	Male	Total
32	18	50	22.5	27.5	50

From the observed and expected frequencies we calculate χ^2 thus:

$$\chi^2 = \frac{(|32 - 22.5| - 0.5)^2}{22.5} + \frac{(|18 - 27.5| - 0.5)^2}{27.5}$$

$$= \frac{81}{22.5} + \frac{81}{27.5}$$

$$\chi^2 = 3.60 + 2.95 = 6.55$$

What does this χ^2 tell us? We see from Table F that to be significant at the 0.01 level, χ^2 must be at least 6.63. The value we have calculated is not quite large enough to be significant at the 0.01 level but is well beyond 3.84, needed for significance at the 0.05 level. We therefore reject the Null Hypothesis and conclude that something other than chance has caused the sample to depart from the probabilities of 0.45 (female) and 0.55 (male).

What might that 'something' be? We cannot be sure. Some of the possibilities we considered earlier when testing the Null Hypothesis that males and females are equally likely to be sampled could apply just as well to this result: the numbers in the population of all passengers may not be those that occur at the particular times when the survey was conducted or Albert and Victoria may not have sampled them at random – and it's possible that both of these explanations contribute to the result.

Why did we get one non-significant result and one significant result from two χ^2 analyses of the same data?

It may surprise you that the same observed frequencies – of male and female passengers in the sample – can give a significant result in one χ^2 analysis but a non-significant result in another. It should not be a surprise, and neither result is 'wrong'. *We have obtained different answers because we have asked two different questions about the data.*

We first asked if such results could reasonably occur if males and females both have a probability of 0.5 of being included in the sample. The answer to that question was, yes. In the second analysis, we asked if such results could reasonably occur if males have a probability of 0.55 and females a probability of 0.45. The answer to that was, no. The large number of females that Albert and Victoria found in their sample is more unlikely if the probability of a female is 0.45 than if it is 0.5, so there is no error here – they are correct answers to different questions.

Sign test (again)

Chi-squared can only be used with numbers that are **frequencies** (numbers of cases): never with actual scores. But raw scores or measurements can, of course, be used to classify things or people into categories, allowing us to count the number of cases in each category. For example, we can count the numbers of passengers who overestimate and underestimate waiting time. If we combine the data in Table 1 (Albert's results) and Table 2 (Victoria's results) we have data on 50 passengers. If we compare their estimated waiting times with their actual waiting times we can see that there were 39 positive differences (overestimates) and 11 negative differences (underestimates).

We can use χ^2 to decide if the difference between the frequencies (numbers) of underestimates and of overestimates is so large that it would be unlikely to occur by chance alone if both kinds of error are equally likely. That is, our Null Hypothesis is: *The probability of overestimates is equal to that of underestimates.*

That Null Hypothesis says nothing about the probability of a passenger's estimate being correct. As it happens, nobody did give a correct estimate of waiting time, but any who had done so would have been dropped from the analysis. That leaves only two possible kinds of estimate, overestimates and underestimates, so the sum of their probabilities must be 1.0 (one or other of them must occur). If both probabilities are the same, they must both be 0.5 to make them add up to 1.0.

Helen Welford

Dividing into categories according to size of score

TABLE 12. Observed and expected frequencies of overestimates and underestimates of waiting time by 50 bus passengers

	Positive differences (Overestimates)	Negative differences (Underestimates)	Total
Observed frequency	39	11	50
Expected frequency	25	25	50

The expected frequencies are found by multiplying the total of the observed frequencies by the probabilities of the two types of error, that is, by 0.5 in each case. Since there are only two observed frequencies (41 and 9), df = 1.

The calculation therefore uses the formula for χ^2, with Yates's correction for continuity:

$$\chi^2 = \frac{(\,|39-25|-0.5\,)^2}{25} + \frac{(\,|11-25|-0.5\,)^2}{25} = 7.29 + 7.29 = 14.58$$

How should the result be interpreted? From Table F we see that with 1 df, χ^2 must be 6.63 or larger to be significant at the 0.01 level. Since it is larger than that, the result is significant at the 0.01 level. We conclude that we are unlikely to get so great a difference between the number of passengers who overestimate and those who underestimate if both types of error are equally likely. Thus there seems to be a real difference in the probability of overestimating and underestimating. We can see from the actual results that overestimating is more probable, but before we saw the data there was no logical reason why it might not have been the opposite, so the test we applied was a *non-directional* (two-tailed) one.

You may have noticed that the conclusion is the same as the one we reached previously when we carried out the sign test on the same data using Table C. In fact the calculation we have carried out here is just another form of the sign test. Table C is preferable if the numbers are small enough to be found in it. However, if the numbers are too large to use Table C, the approximation given by chi-squared is excellent. (This is similar to using z to decide if a Mann-Whitney U is significant when there is a large amount of data.)

Summary

❑ Chi-squared (χ^2) is a statistic that can be used to answer questions about data that consist of *frequencies* of *independent events*.

❑ In a one-sample χ^2 test, the frequencies with which various categories of result are observed to occur (*observed frequencies*, O) are compared with the average frequencies that are expected (*expected frequencies*, E) according to the Null Hypothesis.

❑ A common Null Hypothesis is that all the categories are equally probable.

❑ The degrees of freedom (df) in a one-sample χ^2 test are given by the number of observed frequencies that are free to vary without affecting the expected frequencies. Generally, that is equal to K- 1, where K is the number of categories.

❑ Chi-squared can be used to carry out a sign test if the number of cases is large.

Interpreting the frequencies of categories in two or more samples

KEY AIMS: By the end of Part 6 you should understand:

▷ *how to use the chi-squared statistic to compare the proportion of cases of two or more types in two or more samples;*

▷ *how and when to carry out a median test;*

▷ *what requirements must be fulfilled before a chi-squared test is appropriate.*

Albert: How come you've got so many women in your sample?
Victoria: I don't know. There just seemed to be more of them about.

The chi-squared calculations we made in Part 5 concerned *one sample*, just like the one-sample *t*-test and the Wilcoxon test. There is also a way to use chi-squared if we want to compare *two samples*, corresponding to the two-sample *t*-test and the Mann-Whitney test. For example, we have been assuming until now that Albert and Victoria approached passengers at random, paying attention only to which bus the passenger was waiting for. But maybe that wasn't the case. Maybe, without meaning to, Victoria tended to approach more female passengers and Albert more males, or vice-versa. Is there perhaps a systematic bias here?

Comparing Victoria's sample with Albert's

We can think of the passengers approached by Albert as one sample and those approached by Victoria as another. Albert questioned 26 passengers and Victoria questioned 24. The numbers of male and female passengers questioned by each are shown in Table 13.

TABLE 13. Numbers of male and of female passengers interviewed by Albert and by Victoria (Observed frequencies)

	Albert	Victoria	Total
Males	12	6	18
Females	14	18	32
	26	24	50

Albert questioned a higher proportion of male passengers than Victoria, but is it possible that both have the same *probability* of questioning male and female passengers and the difference in the actual proportions has resulted from chance alone?

The probability of questioning males may not be *equal* to that of questioning females. There were many more female passengers than male passengers in the survey so it seems that females were more likely to be interviewed. We are going to test the following Null Hypothesis: *The probabilities of questioning male and female passengers are the same for Albert as for Victoria.*

© Copyright. No photocopying allowed

Q: If that Null Hypothesis is true, what *are* the probabilities of questioning a male and of questioning a female?

A: Since 18 males were questioned out of the 50 passengers in the survey, the probability of questioning a male is 18/50, or 0.36. The probability of questioning a female is 32/50 or 0.64.

If Victoria and Albert select passengers in the same way, it follows from our Null Hypothesis that both have these probabilities, 0.36 and 0.64.

We can now make a table of expected frequencies by taking account of the probabilities that follow from the Null Hypothesis and the numbers of passengers questioned by Victoria and by Albert. Albert's sample of 26 will thus consist of 26 x 0.36 = 9.36 males and 26 x 0.64 = 16.64 females. Victoria's sample of 24 will consist of 24 x 0.36 = 8.64 males and 24 x 0.64 = 15.36 females. These expected frequencies are shown in Table 14.

TABLE 14. Expected frequencies of male and of female passengers interviewed by Albert and Victoria on the Null Hypothesis that both have the same probabilities of interviewing males and females

	Albert	Victoria	Total
Males	9.36	8.64	18
Females	16.64	15.36	32
	26	24	50

To check how many df there are, note how the expected frequencies were calculated. We obtained the probabilities of males and females from the row totals (18 and 32) and used the numbers in the two samples, shown in the column totals (26 and 24). Thus to leave the expected frequencies unaltered, these row and column totals must not change. What happens if you change just one number in one of the cells of the table? You will find that only *one* number in the table of observed frequencies can be varied: as soon as you change one, all the other numbers have to take particular values if the row and column totals are not to change. Thus there is only 1 df for this χ^2 calculation.

Since there is only 1 df it is safer to use Yates's correction when calculating χ^2:

$$\chi^2 = \Sigma \frac{(|O - E| - 0.5)^2}{E}$$

$$\chi^2 = \frac{(|12 - 9.36| - 0.5)^2}{9.36} + \frac{(|6 - 8.64| - 0.5)^2}{8.64} + \frac{(|14 - 16.64| - 0.5)^2}{16.64}$$

$$+ \frac{(|18 - 15.36| - 0.5)^2}{15.36}$$

$$= 0.489 + 0.530 + 0.275 + 0.298 = 1.592$$

What does the result tell us? Consulting Table F, we find that with 1 df, χ^2 must be 6.63 or greater to be significant at the 0.01 level, and 3.84 or greater to be significant at the 0.05 level. Thus the result of 1.592 is not significant even at the lower level ($p \geq 0.05$). We therefore cannot reject the Null Hypothesis that their probabilities are equal. As always happens with a statistical inference from a non-significant result, we can't conclude that there certainly was no bias, only that the observed results could perfectly well occur even without bias.

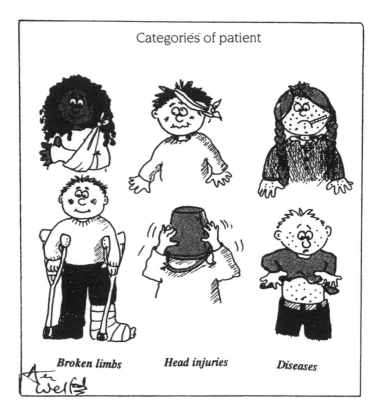

Categories of patient

Broken limbs **Head injuries** **Diseases**

Median test

In Part 5 we saw that it is possible to divide a single sample into two categories according to whether the scores were positive or negative. In a similar way, we can divide *two* samples into categories on the basis of scores, giving us a test for comparing two samples.

If some scores are positive and some are negative, we can test the Null Hypothesis that the probability of positive scores is the same in both samples. More commonly, however, we consider the median of all the scores and test the Null Hypothesis that the probability of exceeding it is the same in both samples, since that can be done even if all scores are positive or all are negative. This is equivalent to testing the Null Hypothesis that *both samples come from populations that have the same median*, so this way of comparing scores is called the **median test.**

To carry out the test, we first calculate the median of all the scores, just as though they formed a single sample. If the Null Hypothesis is true, we expect about half of each sample to lie above that median and half of each sample to lie below it. If, instead, we find that most of one sample lie above it while most of the other sample lie below it, we will conclude that the results do not agree with what the Null Hypothesis predicts. We then reject it in favour of the Alternative Hypothesis. To decide if the difference between what the Null Hypothesis predicts and the results we observed is unusual enough to be significant, we can calculate χ^2 and consult Table F.

An example of the median test

Let's try that approach with the data from Table 6 (estimates of waiting time given by male and female passengers). In Part 4 we tested these results using a two-sample *t*-test and a Mann-Whitney test, and with both we found that the result was significant at the 0.05 level. If we think that either of these tests is appropriate it is not a good idea to use a median test *as well*. It uses even less of the information in the data than the Mann-Whitney does so it is less able to show that effects are significant even when they are real – but, on the other hand, the median test is the easiest to calculate of the three tests so it can be useful if results seem so clear-cut that all we need is a quick and simple test that makes no assumptions about the distribution of scores in the population.

The median score in Table 6 is 10, so all passengers who gave an Estimate of 10 minutes are omitted from the test. The information we use is the number of females and the number of males who made scores above 10 and below 10 and these frequencies are shown in Table 15. After omitting those who gave the median estimate of 10 minutes, we have a sample of 12 female passengers and another of 10 male passengers.

TABLE 15. Observed frequencies of male and female passengers coming above and below the joint median of both groups in the data of Table 6

	Female passengers	Male passengers	Total
Above the median	4	8	12
Below the median	8	2	10
	12	10	22

We are going to test the Null Hypothesis that female and male passengers have the same probability of giving estimates that are above and the same probability of giving estimates that are below that median. But what are these probabilities? They will always be approximately 0.5 since half of all scores lie above the median and half lie below but it may not be exactly 0.5 if several scores in the data are equal.

Here, a total of 12 scores were above the median and 10 scores were below it so the corresponding probabilities of coming above and below the median are $12 \div 22$ or 0.5455 and $10 \div 22$ or 0.4545. The expected frequencies that follow from these probabilities are shown in Table 16:

TABLE 16. Expected frequencies of female and male passengers coming above and below the joint median of both groups on the Null Hypothesis that the probability of coming above and below is the same for males as it is for females

	Female passengers	Male passengers	Total
Above the median	6.55	5.45	12
Below the median	5.45	4.55	10
	14	10	22

How many degrees of freedom are there in a median test? Well, we calculated the probabilities of falling above and below the median from the row totals. We then calculated the expected frequencies by multiplying these probabilities by the numbers in the two samples (the column totals) so none of these totals must change or the expected frequencies will change. As soon as we know one observed frequency, we can work out all the others from the row and column totals, so there is just 1 *df*. The calculation of χ^2, using Yates's correction, is as follows:

$$\chi^2 = \frac{(|4 - 6.55| - 0.5)^2}{6.55} + \frac{(|8 - 5.45| - 0.5)^2}{5.45} + \frac{(|8 - 5.45| - 0.5)^2}{5.45} +$$

$$\frac{(|2 - 4.55| - 0.5)^2}{4.55}$$

$$= 0.642 + 0.771 + 0.771 + 0.924 = 3.108$$

When we consult Table F for 1 df we find that χ^2 needs to be 3.84 or larger to be significant at the 0.05 level. The result here is smaller than that, so the result is not significant at the 0.05 level: the result we obtained is expected to occur more than one time in twenty even if the populations of males and females have the same median.

Answers we obtain by using chi-squared are somewhat unreliable if the amount of data is small, especially if any *expected* frequency is small. A common rule of thumb is that no expected frequency should be less than 5. In the median test we have just carried out, one of the expected frequencies was only 4.55, so the outcome is slightly suspect. However, since our conclusion is that we can not reject the Null Hypothesis, that does not matter much since the outcome is really a failure to reach any firm conclusion.

How does the result compare with those from the *t*-test and the Mann-Whitney test?

Since χ^2 is not significant, we conclude that the difference between the medians of the estimates by the male and female passengers can plausibly be accounted for by chance alone. But when we examined these results in Part 4 we found the result to be significant at the 0.05 level both with the *t*-test and the Mann-Whitney test. We now find that the median test is not significant at the 0.05 level.

That is not a mistake, though. Every statistical test asks a slightly different question and is sensitive to different features of the data. The median test pays no attention to the *amount* by which a score lies above or below the median (which the *t*-test does) nor even to the ranks of the scores (as the Mann-Whitney test does). These tests therefore use more of the information in the data and are better able to demonstrate something to be significant if it really exists. You will recall that a similar relationship held between the sign test and the other tests for one sample.

For a result to be significant with a sign test or a median test it needs to be more clear cut than it does to be significant with a one-sample or two-sample *t*-test, a Mann-Whitney test or a Wilcoxon test, all of which have more power.

Rules for using chi-squared

Although chi-squared is very versatile and generally quite simple to calculate, we must always check that it is appropriate to use it. On the following page are some rules that will help to avoid the most likely errors.

Rule	Notes and Examples
The observed frequencies must be *frequencies*. Do not use scores or measurements.	Numbers of people or numbers of correct and wrong answers are okay. Lengths, times or examination marks are not.
One individual being, or not being, in one of the categories must not affect the probability that another person will fall in a particular category.	For instance, if only married couples are questioned, then selecting any female entails selecting also her husband.
Categories must not overlap. It should not be possible for any item to fall into more than one category at a time.	For instance, it would not be correct to divide passengers into four categories labelled 'male', 'female', 'married' and unmarried'. A passenger in the category 'male', say, would also be in one of the categories 'married' or 'unmarried'.
No individual should contribute more than one unit to the total of the observed frequencies (unless *all* the results relate to the same person).	For example, it would be wrong to have a table of observed frequencies consisting of all the correct and all the wrong answers given on a test by a class of students because each student would contribute several correct and incorrect answers to the total.
The total of the expected frequencies must always equal the total of the observed frequencies.	If it doesn't, some error has been made.
Yates's correction for continuity is used only when there is just 1 degree of freedom.	It has little effect if the frequencies are very large.
None of the *expected* frequencies should be less than 5. (It doesn't matter how small the observed frequencies are.)	The probabilities in tables of χ^2 are based on mathematical approximations that are not accurate if any of the expected frequencies are very small.

For each of the sets of data, (a) to (d) below, write down answers to the following questions.

- Would it be appropriate to calculate χ^2?
- If χ^2 is appropriate, state a Null Hypothesis that might be tested.
- If χ^2 is not appropriate, explain briefly why not.

a) Numbers of students from two classes passing and failing a particular examination.

	Passing	Failing
Class W	25	11
Class X	15	9

b) Marks awarded in a test to the highest and lowest scoring student in each of two classes.

	Highest scoring student	Lowest scoring student
Class Y	85	40
Class Z	70	50

c) Number of days in one week on which John Jones complained of headache.

Headache	No headache
2	5

d) Numbers of white-collar and blue-collar workers in a factory.

	Aged over 30	Aged under 40
White-collar	25	15
Blue-collar	75	130

More than two categories; more than two samples

The approach we have used for two samples, each divided into the same two categories, can be applied to any number of samples and any number of categories. Let's jump now to an example with three samples and four categories – you can then apply the principle to any number of samples or categories you want.

Victoria and Albert had asked a separate and larger group of passengers what they thought about the bus service in general and kept a record of the time of day at which the question was asked in case opinions fluctuated throughout the day. That might occur either because the bus service was better at some times than at others or because passengers tended to be of a different type at certain times – or both might be true. The results of that part of the survey are in Table 17.

We will focus on the question of whether or not the variation from one time of day to another in the opinions expressed can be explained by chance alone. If chance can explain the variation, we need not seek to explain it by differences either in the quality of the service or in the characteristics of the passengers at these times.

SOMETHING TO TRY

Before going on, examine Table 17 and see what you think the answer to that question will be. Then write out a Null Hypothesis (involving probabilities) that accounts for these results by chance alone.

TABLE 17. Distribution of responses to the question 'How satisfied are you with your bus service?' tabulated separately for passengers questioned in the early morning, at midday and in the evening.

	Very satisfied	Fairly satisfied	Fairly dissatisfied	Very dissatisfied	Total
Morning	15	8	10	7	40
Midday	5	13	12	10	40
Evening	10	19	8	3	40
Total	30	40	30	20	120

A suitable Null Hypothesis is: *The probability of each opinion about the bus service is the same in the populations of Morning passengers, Midday passengers and Evening passengers.* According to the Null Hypothesis, the results show different patterns only because three different samples have been drawn at random from populations whose patterns of opinion are identical.

We now calculate a table of Expected Frequencies to reflect that Null Hypothesis. First, we estimate the distribution of the four responses in these populations if the probabilities of the responses do not depend on the time of day. We get that estimate from the total number of each answer: the probability of a 'Very satisfied' response is 30/120 or 0.25; for 'Fairly satisfied' it is 40/120 or 0.333; for 'Fairly dissatisfied' it is 30/120 or 0.25; and for 'Very dissatisfied' it is 20/120 or 0.167.

Now we ask what frequencies we expect if the Null Hypothesis is correct. For those questioned in the Morning, the expected frequencies are found by multiplying the number of passengers in that group (40) by the probability of each of the responses indicated by the Null Hypothesis (0.25, 0.333, 0.25 and 0.167). These expected frequencies are therefore : 40 x 0.25, 40 x 0.333, 40 x 0.25 and 40 x 0.167, or 10, 13.333, 10 and 13.333. The numbers questioned at Midday and in the Evening were also 40, giving the expected frequencies in Table 18.

TABLE 18. Expected frequencies derived from the Null Hypothesis that the probability of each answer in Table 17 does not depend on the time of day it was asked

	Very satisfied	Fairly satisfied	Fairly dissatisfied	Very dissatisfied	Total
Morning	10	13.333	10	6.667	40
Midday	10	13.333	10	6.667	40
Evening	10	13.333	10	6.667	40
Total	30	40	30	20	120

One of the frequencies in Table 17 is only 3. Should that cause concern about the validity of a χ^2 test of significance?

Determining the number of df

Though we have more rows and columns here than we have used before, exactly the same principles give us the number of degrees of freedom. We used the column totals to decide the probability of each response in the population and we multiplied that by the row total (the sample size) to find the expected frequencies in each row. Thus if the expected frequencies are not to change, neither must the row or column totals.

Pick any row. By the time we have filled in three of its numbers, the fourth is fixed by the row total. We can do the same with one further row, but when we have filled two rows like that, the third is completely fixed by the need to make up the columns to the right totals. Thus there are six numbers that can be altered while keeping all the totals fixed. Hence, there are six degrees of freedom for chi-squared.

➤ When the expected frequencies are calculated in exactly the way they were here, there is a simple rule that yields the correct number of degrees of freedom:

In a table with R rows and C columns, df = (R - 1)(C - 1).

In the present case, there are 3 rows and 4 columns, so df = (3 - 1)(4 - 1) = 2 × 3 = 6. This rule is more convenient than thinking about how many observed frequencies are free to vary, but it can not be relied upon. Like the rule, df = K -1, for the one-sample case, it does not reflect the meaning of 'degrees of freedom' and it can give the wrong answer if the Null Hypothesis is unusual.

Because we have more than one df we do not use Yates's correction when calculating χ^2. For each of the twelve cells in Table 17 we subtract the expected frequency shown in the corresponding cell of Table 18, square the difference and divide by the expected frequency. When we add up these twelve answers, the value we get for χ^2 is 14.05. When we consult Table F in the row for 6 df we find that χ^2 must be 12.59 to be significant at the 0.05 level and 16.81 to be significant at the 0.01 level. The result is therefore significant at the 0.05 level.

How should the result be interpreted? The significant χ^2 tells us that chance is not a satisfactory explanation for the different distributions of answers at each time of day. However, it does not tell us what else is responsible for the differences. For example, we still have no way of telling if it should be attributed to variation in the bus service or variation in the passengers. Indeed, it does not even tell us what the differences *are*. For that, we need to examine the data in Table 17.

Perhaps you spotted that the morning and evening passengers were, on the whole, more satisfied than the midday ones. There is also a tendency for the morning passengers to be more extreme in their views than the evening ones. (More of the morning ones were *very* satisfied or *very* dissatisfied.) It is quite possible that other patterns can be seen too, and if so it is up to you to point them out. The χ^2 calculation has done only one job for you – it has eliminated chance as a satisfactory explanation. Unless that can be done, there is not much point in worrying about what other explanations are possible.

Summary

❑ Chi-squared can be used to compare two or more samples to see if the frequencies with which they divide into categories could reasonably result from chance alone.

❑ The degrees of freedom are given by the number of observed frequencies that are free to vary without changing the expected frequencies, and in many cases that is equal to (R-1)(C-1), where R is the number of rows and C is the number of columns.

❑ For a valid chi-squared calculation, the observations must be *frequencies* of *independent events* and none of the *expected* frequencies should be less than 5.

❑ The number of scores above and below the median of all the scores can be used to calculate χ^2 as a test of the null hypothesis that two samples of scores have the same median.

Summary of the statistical methods in this Unit

This Unit has covered several common statistical tests. Once you understand them you will be able to analyse most of the data you generate. But there are dangers in presenting the methods in this concentrated form. Firstly, all of the statistical methods described in this Unit have the objective of eliminating chance as a satisfactory explanation for experimental results by showing that results are *statistically significant*. But we must never lose sight of the fact that tests of significance are pretty useless in isolation. There is little point in showing that a result is significant unless we first show what the result *is*. Results should always be described carefully before any test of significance is invoked. Several methods for doing that are described in Unit 2.

Secondly, in order to demonstrate significance tests, we have often applied several tests to the same set of data. That has been done to illustrate and compare the methods but it is *not* something we would do when analyzing the results of an investigation. As a rule, we should decide in advance on a single analysis appropriate to our particular problem and stick to it. How do we decide? Here are some questions to ask yourself and some advice to follow depending on your answers.

Question	Advice
Are the numbers frequencies (numbers of instances, items or individuals) or scores (measurements)?	If they are frequencies you can often use chi-squared (but it is sometimes possible to treat frequencies as scores and use one of the other methods). If they are scores, you must not use chi-squared.
Do the scores come from two unrelated samples of individuals or from a single sample of individuals? (Two samples of *matched* individuals can be treated in the same way as a single sample.)	With two unrelated samples, you can use the two-sample *t*-test, the Mann-Whitney test or the median test. To compare pairs of scores from a single sample (each person providing two numbers), you can use the one-sample *t*-test, the Wilcoxon test or the sign test.
If the numbers are measurements, do they follow an approximately Normal distribution without serious outliers?	If scores are not distributed approximately Normally, it is safer to use the Wilcoxon test than a one-sample *t*-test and it is even safer to use the sign test. It is safer to use the Mann-Whitney test than a two-sample *t*-test.
Does the difference between the groups of scores appear to be a large one relative to variability in the scores? (In other words, is there little overlap in values between the two sets of scores?)	If so, it may be sufficient to use an insensitive but simple test: the sign test for differences within a single sample or the median test for comparing two samples.
Is the degree of *relationship* between two measurements (such as test score and age) the focus of interest?	Calculate a correlation coefficient (see Unit 2, *Describing and Interpreting Data*).
Are there more than two groups of scores (such as three conditions in an experiment)?	Unless the results are frequencies appropriate for χ^2, you will need methods more advanced than those in this Unit.

© Copyright. No photocopying allowed

Statistical Tables

TABLE A. Values of *t* reaching the 0.05 and 0.01 levels of significance in a non-directional test

Enter the table in the row corresponding to the df in the data. To be significant at the 0.05 level in a non-directional test, *t* must be as great as the value in Column 2, or greater. To be significant at the 0.01 level, *t* must be as great as the value in Column 3, or greater. If the df you want are not present in the table, use the row with the next *smaller* number of df.

| | Significance | |
df	0.05	0.01
1	12.706	63.657
2	4.303	9.925
3	3.182	5.841
4	2.776	4.604
5	2.571	4.032
6	2.447	3.707
7	2.365	3.499
8	2.306	3.355
9	2.262	3.250
10	2.228	3.169
11	2.201	3.106
12	2.179	3.055
13	2.160	3.012
14	2.145	2.977
15	2.131	2.947
16	2.120	2.921
17	2.110	2.898
18	2.101	2.878
19	2.093	2.861
20	2.086	2.845
22	2.074	2.819
24	2.064	2.797
26	2.056	2.779
28	2.048	2.763
30	2.042	2.750
32	2.037	2.738
34	2.032	2.728
36	2.028	2.719
38	2.024	2.712
40	2.021	2.704
50	2.009	2.678
60	2.000	2.660
80	1.990	2.639
100	1.984	2.626
200	1.972	2.601
500	1.965	2.586
1000	1.962	2.581
∞	1.960	2.576

TABLE B. Values of T reaching the 0.05 and 0.01 levels of significance in a non-directional Wilcoxon test

Enter the table in the row corresponding to N (the number of non-zero differences in the data). To be significant at the 0.05 level in a non-directional test, T must be as small as the value in Column 2 or smaller. To be significant at the 0.01 level, T must be as small as the value in Column 3 or smaller. If N is less than 8 it is not possible for a result to be significant at the 0.01 level and if N is less than 6 it can not be significant at the 0.05 level either.

| | Significance | |
N	0.05	0.01
6	0	—
7	2	—
8	3	0
9	5	2
10	8	3
11	10	5
12	13	7
13	17	10
14	21	13
15	25	16
16	29	20
17	34	23
18	40	28
19	46	32
20	52	38
21	58	43
22	65	49
23	73	55
24	81	61
25	89	68
26	98	75
27	107	83
28	116	91
29	126	100
30	137	109

Table B is adapted from McCormack, R. L. (1965). Extended tables of the Wilcoxon matched pair signed rank statistic. *Journal of the American Statistical Association*, 60, 864-871. Reprinted with permission from the *Journal of the American Statistical Association*. Copyright 1965 by the American Statistical Association. All rights reserved.

TABLE C. Values of the Sign Test statistic reaching the 0.05 and 0.01 levels of significance in a non-directional test.

Enter the table in the row corresponding to N (the number of non-zero differences in the data). To be significant at the 0.05 level in a non-directional test, the smaller number of signs (+ or -) must be the same as the value in Column 2 or smaller. To be significant at the 0.01 level, the smaller number of signs must be the same as the value in Column 3 or smaller. If N is less than 8 it is not possible for a result to be significant at the 0.01 level and if N is less than 6 it can not be significant at the 0.05 level either.

| | Significance | |
N	0.05	0.01
6	0	—
7	0	—
8	0	0
9	1	0
10	1	0
11	1	0
12	2	1
13	2	1
14	2	1
15	3	2
16	3	2
17	4	2
18	4	3
19	4	3
20	5	3
21	5	4
22	5	4
23	6	4
24	6	5
25	7	5
26	7	6
27	7	6
28	8	6
29	8	7
30	9	7
31	9	7
32	9	8
33	10	8
34	10	9
35	12	10
36	12	10
37	13	10
38	13	11
39	13	11
40	14	12

TABLE D. Values of U reaching the 0.05 level of significance in a non-directional Mann-Whitney test.

Enter the table in the row corresponding to the number of cases in one sample, and the column corresponding to the number of cases in the other sample. To be significant at the 0.05 level in a non-directional test, U must be the same as the value in the table or smaller.

Size of Sample B	Size of Sample A																
	4	5	6	7	8	9	10	11	12	13	14	15	16	17	18	19	20
4	0	1	2	3	4	4	5	6	7	8	9	10	11	11	12	13	14
5	1	2	3	5	6	7	8	9	11	12	13	14	15	17	18	19	20
6	2	3	5	6	8	10	11	13	14	16	17	19	21	22	24	25	27
7	3	5	6	8	10	12	14	16	18	20	22	24	26	28	30	32	34
8	4	6	8	10	13	15	17	19	22	24	26	29	31	34	36	38	41
9	4	7	10	12	15	17	20	23	26	28	31	34	37	39	42	45	48
10	5	8	11	14	17	20	23	26	29	33	36	39	42	45	48	52	55
11	6	9	13	16	19	23	26	30	33	37	40	44	47	51	55	58	62
12	7	11	14	18	22	26	29	33	37	41	45	49	53	57	61	65	69
13	8	12	16	20	24	28	33	37	41	45	50	54	59	63	67	72	76
14	9	13	17	22	26	31	36	40	45	50	55	59	64	69	74	78	83
15	10	14	19	24	29	34	39	44	49	54	59	64	70	75	80	85	90
16	11	15	21	26	31	37	42	47	53	59	64	70	75	81	86	92	98
17	11	17	22	28	34	39	45	51	57	63	69	75	81	87	93	99	105
18	12	18	24	30	36	42	48	55	61	67	74	80	86	93	99	106	112
19	13	19	25	32	38	45	52	58	65	72	78	85	92	99	106	113	119
20	14	20	27	34	41	48	55	62	69	76	83	90	98	105	112	119	127

Table D is adapted from Milton, R. C. (1964). An extended table of critical values for the Mann-Whitney (Wilcoxon) two-sample statistic. *Journal of the American Statistical Association* 59, 925-934. Reprinted with permission from the *Journal of the American Statistical Association*. Copyright 1964 by the American Statistical Association. All rights reserved.

TABLE E. Values of U reaching the 0.01 level of significance in a non-directional Mann-Whitney test.

Enter the table in the row corresponding to the number of cases in one sample, and the column corresponding to the number of cases in the other sample. To be significant at the 0.01 level in a non-directional test, U must be the same as the value in the table or smaller. When there are fewer than 10 cases in total, no result can be significant at the 0.01 level.

Size of Sample A

Size of Sample B	4	5	6	7	8	9	10	11	12	13	14	15	16	17	18	19	20
4	-	-	0	0	1	1	2	2	3	3	4	5	5	6	6	7	8
5	-	0	1	1	2	3	4	5	6	7	7	8	9	10	11	12	13
6	0	1	2	3	4	5	6	7	9	10	11	12	13	15	16	17	18
7	0	1	3	4	6	7	9	10	12	13	15	16	18	19	21	22	24
8	1	2	4	6	7	9	11	13	15	17	18	20	22	24	26	28	30
9	1	3	5	7	9	11	13	16	18	20	22	24	27	29	31	33	36
10	2	4	6	9	11	13	16	18	21	24	26	29	31	34	37	39	42
11	2	5	7	10	13	16	18	21	24	27	30	33	36	39	42	45	48
12	3	6	9	12	15	18	21	24	27	31	34	37	41	44	47	51	54
13	3	7	10	13	17	20	24	27	31	34	38	42	45	49	53	57	60
14	4	7	11	15	18	22	26	30	34	38	42	46	50	54	58	63	67
15	5	8	12	16	20	24	29	33	37	42	46	51	55	60	64	69	73
16	5	9	13	18	22	27	31	36	41	45	50	55	60	65	70	74	79
17	6	10	15	19	24	29	34	39	44	49	54	60	65	70	75	81	86
18	6	11	16	21	26	31	37	42	47	53	58	64	70	75	81	87	92
19	7	12	17	22	28	33	39	45	51	57	63	69	74	81	87	93	99
20	8	13	18	24	30	36	42	48	54	60	67	73	79	86	92	99	105

Table E is adapted from Milton, R. C. (1964). An extended table of critical values for the Mann-Whitney (Wilcoxon) two-sample statistic. *Journal of the American Statistical Association*, 59, 925–934. Reprinted with permission from the *Journal of the American Statistical Association*. Copyright 1964 by the American Statistical Association. All rights reserved.

TABLE F. Values of chi-squared reaching the 0.05 and 0.01 levels of significance in a non-directional test

Enter the table in the row corresponding to the df in the data. To be significant at the 0.05 level in a non-directional test, χ^2 must be as great as the value in Column 2 or greater. To be significant at the 0.01 level, χ^2 must be as great as the value in Column 3 or greater.

| | Significance | |
df	0.05	0.01
1	3.84	6.63
2	5.99	9.21
3	7.81	11.34
4	9.49	13.28
5	11.07	15.09
6	12.59	16.81
7	14.07	18.48
8	15.51	20.09
9	16.92	21.67
10	18.31	23.21
11	19.68	24.72
12	21.03	26.22
13	22.36	27.69
14	23.68	29.14
15	25.00	30.58
16	26.30	32.00
17	27.59	33.41
18	28.87	34.81
19	30.14	36.19
20	31.41	37.57
22	33.92	40.29
24	36.42	42.98
26	38.89	45.64
28	41.34	48.28
30	43.77	50.89
32	46.19	53.49
34	48.60	56.06
36	51.00	58.62
38	53.38	61.16
40	55.76	63.69

GLOSSARY

Aggregate conclusion: an answer which is true on average but is not necessarily true of every individual. See also 'General conclusion'.

Assume: take to be true without evidence, or with very inadequate evidence.

Alternative Hypothesis: the logical opposite of the **Null Hypothesis**, asserting that those things the Null Hypothesis says are false are true, and that those things the Null Hypothesis says are true are false. Equivalent to **Experimental Hypothesis.**

Bias: any tendency for results to differ from the true value in some *consistent* way. Bias should be distinguished from random error, which does not occur in any particular direction.

Chi-squared: The expected distribution of the **sum of squares** for scores distributed according to the **normal curve**. The symbol for a **statistic** calculated in such a way that it is expected to follow the chi-squared distribution is the squared Greek letter Chi (χ^2). The statistic is used in various tests based on the **frequencies** with which events occur.

Correlation coefficient: a number between −1 and +1 indicating the strength and direction of any tendency for the size of score on one variable to be related to the size of score on another.

Degrees of freedom (df): the number of different ways in which scores are free to vary around some value (such as their mean).

Deviation: the difference between an individual score and the mean of the group of scores it belongs to.

Directional test: a **statistical test** in which any difference – however large – in one direction is attributed to chance and the **Null Hypothesis** is not rejected. If the results show a difference in the opposite direction, the result may be significant. The terms **one-tailed** and 'one-sided 'are equivalent. The alternative possibility is a **non-directional** (or 'two-tailed' or 'two-sided')test where a difference in either direction can constitute evidence against the Null Hypothesis.

Distribution: the relative **frequencies** with which scores of different sizes occur.

Distribution-dependent test: see **distribution-free test.**

Distribution-free test: a statistical test that makes no assumption about the shape of the distribution of random errors. As a result, such a test gives valid results when we are uncertain about the nature of the distribution or where the data indicate that the distribution is not the one assumed by a **distribution-dependent** test such as the **t-test**. Compared with a distribution-dependent test, a distribution-free test such as the **Mann-Whitney** usually has less statistical power but can be used with confidence in more cases. The terms 'non-parametric' and 'parametric' are often used as synonyms for 'distribution-free' and distribution-dependent'.

Expected frequencies: in a chi-squared test, the mean values of the **frequencies** that would occur if the **Null Hypothesis** is true and data-collection is repeated many times.

Experimental design: the activity of planning data collection (generally, but not always, an **experiment)** in such a way as to make it possible for the results to be interpreted as clearly and efficiently as possible.

Experimental Hypothesis: See **Alternative Hypothesis.**

Frequency: describes the number of times that something occurs, for example the number of scores that have a particular size.

General conclusion: an answer which is true of every individual. See also 'Aggregate conclusion'.

Hypothesis: a prediction or an explanation that is considered to be possible but is not known to be correct. See also **Alternative Hypothesis** and **Null Hypothesis.**

Inference: a conclusion reached by a process of calculation or logical deduction.

Mann-Whitney test: A **distribution-free** test for two groups of unmatched scores.

Median test: a **distribution-free** significance test of the **Null Hypothesis** that two populations of scores have the same median.

Non-directional test: See **directional test.**

Non parametric test: any statistical test that does not involve calculating the values of attributes (called parameters) such as the mean and the standard deviation of distributions of scores. The term is often considered equivalent to **distribution-free** test.

Normal curve: a bell-shaped mathematical curve which is important in statistics because it is the distribution expected when a large number of independent causes add together to produce an outcome. As a result, many attributes of humans and animals, such as their heights and weights, have **distributions** that approximately follow a normal curve. (Also known as the **Normal Distribution**)

Null hypothesis: a statistical model which attributes the observed results to chance alone. The probability of obtaining such results if the Null Hypothesis is correct is called the 'significance' of the results. If the probability is small (by convention, anything less than 0.05) the result is said to be 'significant' and the Null Hypothesis is rejected in favour of some other model which attributes at least part of the effect to something other than chance. See **significance test** and **statistical significance.**

Null model: another term for the **Null Hypothesis.**

Observed frequencies: See **expected frequencies.**

One-sample t-test: A *t*-test for discovering the significance of the departure of the mean of a single sample of scores from some specified value. It can also be used to discover if the differences between pairs of scores from matched individuals have a mean differing significantly from zero and when used in that way is usually called a **related t-test.**

One-tailed test: See **directional test.**

Outlier: a score so different from the pattern of the other scores that we suspect it of arising in a different way from the others.

Parameter: an element of a Statistical model. The term is often applied to an attribute of a **population**, such as its mean, whereas the mean of a **sample** of scores is called a **statistic.**

Parametric test: any statistical test relating to attributes (called parameters) such as the mean and the standard deviation of distributions of scores. The **t-test** is a parametric test. See **Distribution-free test.**

Population: a group to which the results of an investigation are intended to apply. Studies typically investigate smaller groups, called **samples** drawn from the appropriate population. A population need not include every individual in a country; we can quite well speak of the population of ten-year-old girls, for example.

Power: the ability of a statistical test to reject the Null Hypothesis when it is false. Some tests have more power than others when used with the same data, but all tests increase in power as the amount of data is increased.

Probability: a number between 0 and 1 which expresses how likely it is that some event will occur. If the probability is near 0, the event is unlikely. If the probability is near 1, the event is almost certain to occur.

Ranks: numbers 1, 2, 3, and so on, often used in place of measurements that have been made on an ordinal scale. Ranks are allocated so that the smallest score gets the rank 1, the next is 2, and so on. If two or more scores are equal, all of them are given the average of the ranks they would have had if they had been slightly different from each other

Related t-test: See **one-sample t-test**

Sample: a smaller group selected for study from a larger group, called a **population,** to which there results are intended to apply.

Sign test: a **distribution-free** test of the **Null Hypothesis** that differences between two populations of paired scores (or between one population of scores and a particular value) are equally likely to be positive and negative.

Significance test: equivalent to **Statistical test**. a calculation of the probability of obtaining results such as those observed if the Null Hypothesis is true. If the probability is less than 0.05, the result is said to be significant and we reject the Null Hypothesis as an adequate explanation for the results. When that happens, the Alternative Hypothesis is preferred to the Null Hypothesis that there is no difference.

Significant: See **statistical significance**.

Standard error: a measure of our certainty about the value of some parameter (such as the mean of a distribution). It is equivalent to the standard deviation of our estimate of the parameter. The larger the standard error, the more uncertain we are about the true value of the parameter.

Standard Score: the **deviation** of a score divided by the **Standard Deviation** of the group of scores it belongs to. It is also called **z-score** because z is the usual symbol for a standard score.

Statistic: a numerical value calculated from data to represent some property of the data. For example, a mean and a **correlation coefficient** are statistics. See also **test statistic** and 'Parameter'.

Statistical inference: reaching probabilistic conclusions based on the statistical analysis of data.

Statistical significance: a conclusion that results like those observed have little probability of occurring by chance alone. By convention, results are usually regarded as statistically significant if the probability is less than 0.05 (1 in 20). If a result is statistically significant we feel fairly confident that something other than chance is needed to explain it but we may not know what the 'something' is. Nor does it necessarily follow that the result is of any theoretical or practical importance.

Statistical table: a table of values of a statistic, often showing the size that it needs to be for the result of a **statistical test** to be **significant**.

Statistical test: equivalent to **significance test**.

Sum of squares: the sum of the squares of the **deviations** of a set of scores around their mean. When divided by the **degrees of freedom** (df), it gives an estimate of the standard deviation of the **population** the scores were drawn from.

t- test: a **parametric** and **distribution-dependent** test of the **Null Hypothesis** that two populations of scores follow the normal distribution and have the same mean, or that one normally-distributed population of scores has a particular mean. The simplest form of t-test also assumes, if there are two populations, that they have the same standard deviation.

Test statistic: a **statistic** whose value determines if the result of a statistical test is significant.

Two-sample t-test: a t-test for comparing two groups of unmatched (independent) scores.

Two-tailed test: See **non-directional test**.

Type 1 error: concluding that the Null Hypothesis is false when, in fact, it is true.

Type 2 error: failing to conclude that the Null Hypothesis is false when, in fact, it is false. (Note that we never conclude that the Null Hypothesis is *true*.)

Wilcoxon test: a **non-parametric** and **distribution-free** significance test based on the ranks of the differences between two sets of related scores. It is used with scores which are in pairs (two scores from each participant, for instance).

Yates's correction for continuity: a modification to the calculation of the χ^2 statistic calculated from frequencies which is appropriate only when it has one **degree of freedom**. It takes account of the fact that frequencies must be whole numbers whereas the **chi-squared distribution** is a continuous mathematical function.

z-score: See **standard score**

ANSWERS TO SELF-ASSESMENT QUESTIONS

SAQ 1 (a) The consequences of failing to issue a gale warning are very serious: lives may be lost. It is undesirable to issue a gale warning mistakenly (since it may cause inconvenience and annoyance) but the consequences are not nearly so serious. The meteorologist should be willing to make some Type 1 errors (give warnings that turn out to be false alarms) in order to minimize Type 2 errors (failing to warn of gales that do occur). To achieve that, the significance level should be set at a fairly large probability (0.05 or even larger).

(b) The consequences of failing to publish the article are not very serious: the scientist will have wasted the effort put into the new analysis – and if the results in question are indeed fraudulent, other people may be misled by them. On the other hand, to falsely accuse a colleague of dishonesty may have very serious consequences. Therefore, the scientist needs to be almost certain that a Type 1 error is not occurring so the significance level should be set to a very small probability (0.01, or even less).

SAQ 2 When we make a Type 1 error, we reject the Null Hypothesis (decide that it is wrong), even though it is in fact correct, so our conclusion is mistaken. When we make a Type 2 error we do not reach any definite conclusion – although the Null Hypothesis is in fact false, we decide that the evidence is not strong enough to reject it, but we do *not* mistakenly conclude that it is true.

SAQ 3 (a) A statistical test of this question should be non-directional. If the cat does have a preference, there is no logical reason why she should not prefer to return through the same door.

(b) The cat is as likely to return through the door she left by as through the other door so the probability of returning through the same door is 0.5.

(c) The probability that she will return through the same door is not 0.5. (It may be either greater or smaller.)

SAQ 4 (a) The Null Hypothesis should be non-directional. Even though you expect to have improved by practice, there are perfectly plausible reasons why your score today might be lower than on the day you began training. For example, you might be unwell or off form today.

(b) The best Null Hypothesis to test is that the probability of getting your shots in is the same today as it was at the start of your current training.

(c) Because the test gave a significant result we can reject the Null Hypothesis that your probability of scoring is the same today as at the start. Because the proportion of successes is higher today, you can conclude that you have improved. Note that the conclu-

sion that you have *improved* can be reached only by examining the data: the statistical test says that there is a *difference* but does not tell us its direction.

(d) The conclusion is aggregate, like any result from a significance test. That is, it does not guarantee that now you will *invariably* have a higher proportion of successful shots than you did before training.

SAQ 5 There are four differences of 3 and none of -3. Since they come after eight differences of 1 or -1 and three of 2 or -2, they would have ranks of 12, 13, 14 and 15 if they were slightly different. Since they were all the same, they get the average of these ranks, which is 13.5.

SAQ 6 (a) If the probabilities of being opposed and in favour are equal, each must be 0.5. Therefore, in a sample of 40 people, we expect 20 to be opposed and 20 to be in favour of the plan.

(b) Since the expected frequencies depend on the sample size (40), it must not change. If we know how many are in favour we can deduce how many are opposed, so there is 1 df.

(c) With 1 df, any χ^2 of 6.63 or greater is significant at the 0.01 level, so the result is one that will occur by chance less than one time in a hundred if favourable and unfavourable opinions are equally likely. From the data, we see that most of those in the sample were in favour of the plan, and since the result is significant we can conclude that to be true also of the population they were drawn from. But that population corresponds to *the actual population of the area* only if the reporter selected an unbiased sample of residents.

SAQ 7 (a) Yes. It would be appropriate to test the Null Hypothesis that the probabilities of passing and failing are the same for class X as they are for class W.

(b) No. Marks can not be used. They are not frequencies of independent events.

(c) No. The data are frequencies but they are not independent – if John has a headache on Tuesday he may be more likely to have one on Wednesday too. Also, the expected frequencies could not *both* be 5 or greater since their total is only 7.

(d) No. Although the data are frequencies, the categories overlap. Anyone aged from 31 to 39 would be over 30 and also under 40 and consequently would appear in two categories.

SAQ 8 No. Having small *observed* frequencies does not matter – they can even be zero. What χ^2 requires is that the *expected* frequencies are all 5 or more.